Also by this author

Western Mexico, a Traveler's Treasury

Lake Chapala Through the Ages, an anthology of travelers' tales

Geo-Mexico, the geography and dynamics of modern Mexico
(co-authored with Richard Rhoda, PhD)

MEXICAN KALEIDOSCOPE
myths, mysteries and mystique

MEXICAN KALEIDOSCOPE
myths, mysteries and mystique

TONY BURTON

illustrated by
ENRIQUE VELÁZQUEZ

SB

SOMBRERO BOOKS, B.C., CANADA

Library and Archives Canada Cataloguing in Publication

Burton, Tony, 1953-, author
    Mexican kaleidoscope : myths, mysteries and mystique
/ Tony Burton ; illustrated by Enrique Velázquez.

Includes bibliographical references and index.
Issued in print and electronic formats.
ISBN 978-0-9735191-9-8 (paperback).--ISBN 978-0-9952889-0-4
(ebook)

1. Mexico. 2. Mexico--History. 3. Mexico--Civilization.
4. Mexico--Social life and customs. I. Title.

F1208.B878 2016   972   C2016-906028-4
                                      C2016-906029-2

ISBN 978-0-9735191-9-8
First edition 2016
Text © 2016 by Tony Burton
Illustrations © 2016 by Enrique Velázquez
Cover artwork: Enrique Velázquez

Sombrero Books, Box 4, Ladysmith B.C. V9G 1A1, Canada

Contents

People and society

Culture and beliefs

Preface

My quest to find evidence of the past in Mexico's present led me to some surprising discoveries. Expect the unexpected in this eclectic collection of short chapters. Each of them considers little-known facts, incidents or individuals plucked from the vaults of Mexican heritage. All of these characters and events are part of the kaleidoscope of history that helped shape the country.

The book spans more than 10,000 years of Mexican history from well before the Aztecs through to colonial times, the Mexican Revolution and into this century. While the chapters are grouped into approximate chronological sequence, they can be read in any order.

By looking at myths and mysteries, as well as at conflicting interpretations and opinions, this book offers intriguing insights into the mystique of Mexico, and just why it can rightly be considered one of the most fascinating countries in the world.

Turn the page and join me on a leisurely idiosyncratic stroll through Mexico's colorful kaleidoscopic history and culture.

Before the Spaniards

1

The Three Sisters and early kitchens

Mexican cuisine is one of the country's most successful cultural exports ever. Most large towns in North America and Europe boast at least one Mexican restaurant, even if the menu is not necessarily authentic. The basic ingredients for home-cooked Mexican meals are on the shelves of supermarkets virtually everywhere. The popularity of Mexican food is rivaled only by the demand for Mexican beer, tequila and other drinks.

Archaeologists have also taken much more interest in Mexican food and have made some surprising discoveries. By 1970, studies at various locations, ranging from Tamaulipas in the north of the country to Oaxaca in the south, had led them to conclude that the first plants to be domesticated in Mesoamerica were corn, beans and squash (the Three Sisters), and that all three were domesticated between about 7000 and 10,000 years ago.

Further research subsequently led many paleobotanists to believe that squash was actually domesticated much earlier than corn. Re-evaluating cave samples, originally collected in the 1950s and using an improved carbon-14 dating technique, anthropologist Bruce Smith found that the squash seeds from one location were between 8000 and 10,000 years old, while the oldest corn and bean seeds were much younger, less than 6000 years old.

While Smith's study appears to confirm that squash was domesticated first, it does not necessarily mean that this squash was domesticated for its food value. Some experts contend that early varieties of squash were domesticated primarily for their gourds, which could be used as ready-made drinking vessels and fishing floats.

The domestication of squash may have improved life, but it did not fundamentally change it. On the other hand, the domestication of corn, about 7000 years ago, marked a true watershed in pre–Hispanic life, enabling the abandonment of a nomadic hunter-gatherer existence in favor of settlement in permanent or semi-permanent villages. How important was this? In the words of renowned archaeologist Michael Coe, "it was the cultivation of maize, beans and squash that made possible all of the higher cultures of Mexico."

The Three Sisters are easy to grow together. The maize stems provide climbing support for fast-growing beans. The beans fix nitrogen in the soil, increasing its fertility, while squash plants provide surface cover, outcompeting weeds, creating a moisture-rich microclimate and acting as a living mulch. Maize and beans form the basis of a remarkably balanced, nutritious and healthy diet. Maize lacks the amino acids the human body needs to make proteins and niacin, but these missing amino acids are supplied by beans.

With the passing of time, the ancient peoples of Mexico domesticated and cultivated many other native plants, including tomatoes, chiles, potatoes, avocados, guavas, papayas, amaranth, vegetable pear (chayote), peanuts, vanilla, cacao, cotton and tobacco. In some regions, they also domesticated dogs, rabbits and turkeys for their meat.

Knowing what foodstuffs were available is only one piece of the puzzle. What do we know about how the foods were prepared, or which ones were commonly consumed? Fortunately, archaeologists have increasingly been turning their attention away from how the upper classes lived (and ruled) to focus on the day-to-day lives of the ordinary residents: the farmers, hunters and craftspeople.

Some of the most remarkable studies have been those conducted at Teotihuacan, an hour's drive north of Mexico City, where the Pyramids of the Sun and the Moon were first opened to the public in 1910, just in time for celebrating Mexico's centenary of independence.

At its height (AD450), Teotihuacan was one of the largest cities in the world, with an estimated population of 200,000. Its elaborate water supply, drainage systems and precisely-aligned street grid demonstrate masterful urban planning. The city was so prominent that it became a magnet for craftsmen from other faraway regions like Oaxaca and the Gulf Coast (Veracruz). These migrants would have brought their own food ideas and preferences with them, making Teotihuacan an excellent choice for a cosmopolitan eating experience.

What most present-day visitors to this ancient city are unable to appreciate is how the average Teotihuacanos lived, how they cooked, and what they ate. Cleverly conceived fieldwork between 1985 and 1988 by a team directed by Linda Manzanilla of the National University (UNAM) has unearthed a wealth of information about food storage, preparation methods and kitchens dating back 1500 years.

Manzanilla demonstrated that the exact location of sixth-century kitchens in Teotihuacan can be pinpointed by a combination of traditional and modern archaeological methods. The long-established methods included collecting artifacts, debris, pollen and food remains; their modern counterparts involved the microscopic and chemical analysis of the stucco floors in the multi-room apartment complexes used as residences and workshops.

Soil samples were taken from each square meter of floor and analyzed for certain key indicators. It was already known that, over time, the stucco used on floors absorbed trace amounts of chemicals that indicate the main activities carried out in the room.

High levels of phosphates revealed areas where organic refuse was abundant. This could either be a place where food was consumed or where refuse was discarded. An elevated level of carbonates was assumed to reflect either a place where stucco was processed or somewhere where tortillas were prepared. The tortilla-making process today still involves the liberal application of lime. A localized higher alkaline reading from the stucco floor was correlated to the location of heat or fire. The color of the soil samples was also checked for any indication of the limits of a particular activity.

Once an outline of the distribution of particular activities had been sketched out, the presence of sodium and iron was investigated. High levels of iron, for example, probably indicate where agave was processed or where animals were butchered.

The end result? By correlating the various lines of evidence from this particular sixth-century apartment, Manzanilla was able to pinpoint the precise locations of many everyday household functions. For instance, three areas where ceramic stoves once stood were distinguished. Each had a dark red stain on the floor, with relatively low carbonate values, relatively high alkalinity, and some ash. Significantly higher phosphate values in a band around this zone suggested an area used for eating. Higher phosphate levels were also encountered where any refuse had been swept or accumulated outside the dwelling.

And what was cooked on these stoves? The available evidence suggests that the residents of Teotihuacan had a varied diet of plants and animals. They not only prepared corn, beans, squash and chiles, but also ate prickly pear cacti, potatoes, hawthorns and cherries. For additional protein, rabbits, deer, duck, dogs, turkeys and fish were all on the menu, at least occasionally.

Lest you think their likely diet sounds too bland, the locals also had access to a plethora of herbs and spices, as well as chocolate, chewing gum and tobacco to satisfy their cravings, and various exotic hallucinogens to stimulate their imaginations.

In 2010 the traditional Mexican cuisine of Michoacán was added to UNESCO's list of the Intangible Cultural Heritage of Humanity, on account of the multiple uses and cultural centrality of corn in Mexican traditional cooking. Next time you are eating Mexican food, pause for a moment and remember that your meal may be startlingly similar to the typical dishes eaten thousands of years ago in any major Aztec, Maya or Toltec city.

2

Ancient astronomers rebooted the calendar

Several ancient civilizations developed astonishingly accurate calendars. Even so, occasional adjustments were needed to bring the calendar back in line with solar events.

Some archaeologists studying the site of Xochicalco, near the city of Cuernavaca in central Mexico, believe that a major conference of astronomers was held there in the eighth century AD in order to implement an adjustment of six days. The conference may have been a follow-up to an earlier astronomical gathering (AD700) held in Copán, in modern-day Honduras, commemorated at that site by a richly-decorated altar. An altar may have been good enough for Copán, but in Xochicalco the organizers went one stage further and built an entire, lavishly-decorated pyramid as a memorial to the event.

By the middle of the eighth century, the astronomers of Copán had worked out that the solar year lasted 365.2420 days. This is amazingly close to the modern calculation of 365.2422 days, and superior to the calculations behind either the currently used Gregorian calendar (365.2425 days) or earlier Julian calendar (365.2500 days).

At Xochicalco, the scenic and imposing ruins visible today reflect only a small part of what was formerly a much more extensive city. The name means "place of the home of the flowers", and perhaps Xochicalco was once a flower-bedecked city, but nowadays its flattened hilltop platforms are decidedly semiarid in character. Numerous constructions, linked by cobblestone tracks, rise above the platforms; they include palaces, temples, ballcourts and more than one "observatory" for stargazing.

The central plaza is graced by the amazing Pyramid of the Plumed Serpents. Relatively small (only about six meters tall), it has two levels and may have been roofed at one time. Its *talud y tablero* style, with its gently sloping lower section surmounted by a vertically-sided panel or table, echoes many of the buildings at Teotihuacan. This is probably no accident. Researchers believe that Xochicalco, first settled around AD200, reached its peak only after the decline of the influential city of Teotihuacan, which at its height in around AD450 was one of the world's largest cities.

The Pyramid of the Plumed Serpents (*Pirámide de Quet- zalcóatl*) derives its name from a series of eight plumed stone serpents that wind around its base. Their sinuous bodies frame magnificently adorned seated figures. The serpents appear to be swallowing sun disks: a reference to solar eclipses. Traces of origi- nal pigment show that the panels were once colored. The details of jewelry, shields and headdresses suggest the figures represent high-standing officials of some kind, perhaps the astronomers themselves. The second level of the pyramid is decorated with pairs of seated figures.

Close examination reveals that the styles of the figures on each side of the pyramid are very different. The styles reflect four different major regional cultural groups of the time: the Maya (southern Mexico and neighboring countries), the Zapotec (Oaxaca Valley), the Teotihuacanos (central Mexico) and the Totonac (Gulf coast of Mexico). Presumably, astronomers from all four cultures met here (on neutral territory?) and this unusual monument was built to commemorate their success in finding a solution to a calendar that had become out of sync with the natural year.

According to Roberto Salido Beltrán, this calendric fix was to suppress six days—from day 1-Casa (1-House) to day 11-Mono (11-Monkey)—of the calendar used at that time. As his main evidence, Salido cites a glyph centered on the sign for a house. Two hands reach out from this glyph. The right hand, fingers outstretched, rests on a block. The left hand holds a cord leading to the glyph for 11-Monkey. In terms of our calendar, this event occurred in AD765.

Xochicalco remained prominent until about AD1000, after which it was abandoned. When the Spaniards arrived in the 16th century, they learned of the ruins, but had no inkling of their astronomical significance.

In the past forty years or so, several other major findings have arisen from studies of Xochicalco's astronomical importance. The site lies at a latitude of 18°47" North. At this latitude, the sun is at its zenith (highest point, exactly overhead at midday) on 15 May and 28 July. It is well documented that observing (and celebrating) the solar zenith was very important throughout Mexico at the time the Spaniards arrived, even though modern attempts to revive the ancient practices have not met with much success.

The most magnificent of the site's three ballcourts (the number of ballcourts is a clear indication of how important this site once was) is aligned almost exactly east-west, closely in line with the sun's course on equinox days at this latitude.

Two of the many natural underground caves at Xochicalco show clear evidence of architectural modification, including the perforation of an artificial hole or "chimney" from the cave to the ground above. These vertical shafts would have enabled very precise observations and measurements of solar and possibly planetary events. For instance, the vertical north side of the five-meter-long chimney down into one cave would have resulted in a precisely vertical beam of sunlight on the day of the zenith. The south side of the chimney slopes at an angle of 4°23'. Is it simply a coincidence that this is the exact angle for light to be parallel to this side on 21 June, the day of the Summer solstice? Archeo-astronomers think not!

The dimensions and geometry of this chimney ensure that some light enters the cave every day from 30 April (15 days before the first of the two annual zeniths) to 12 August (15 days after the second). Put another way, the cave receives light every day from precisely 52 days before the solstice to 52 days after it. The number 52 was of immense significance in the pre–Columbian calendar, since it took exactly 52 solar years (18,980 days) for both the solar calendar and the ritual calendar (of 260 days) to return simultaneously to the equivalent of 0-0.

Another fascinating finding, made by Ruben Morante, is that on zenith days, viewed from the "Acropolis" of the site, the sun rises exactly behind Popocatepetl volcano on the eastern horizon. This effect cannot be seen even one day before or after the zenith. The oft-polluted skies over central Mexico mean that relatively few people have been lucky enough to witness this effect.

The evidence from Xochicalco suggests that this archaeological site hosted one of the most important scientific summits ever held in the history of the Americas. The congress of Central American astronomers that met to agree the calendric correction was a landmark event in the history of science worldwide.

Xochicalco is an enthralling place to stroll around, especially if you let your imagination wander. Imagine the astronomers and their cohorts engaged in deep scientific and philosophical discussions. How many days do we need to skip in order to correct the calendar? How are we going to convince the general populace that a reboot is needed?

Visitors will find an excellent small museum, which helps explain the site's significance. The site museum is noteworthy. Designed by Mexican architect Rolando J. Dada y Lemus, it is quite possibly the world's earliest fully sustainable museum, employing solar power, thermal ventilation, collecting rainwater, and irrigating its garden with treated waste water. It opened in 1996, three years before Xochicalco's designation as a UNESCO World Heritage Site.

Xochicalco is 90 kilometers south of Mexico City, 38 kilometers (24 miles) south-west of Cuernavaca. Like other government-run sites, there is a modest entrance fee, except on Sundays and public holidays when access is free. Regular sound and light (*luz y sonido*) shows are scheduled during the winter dry season.

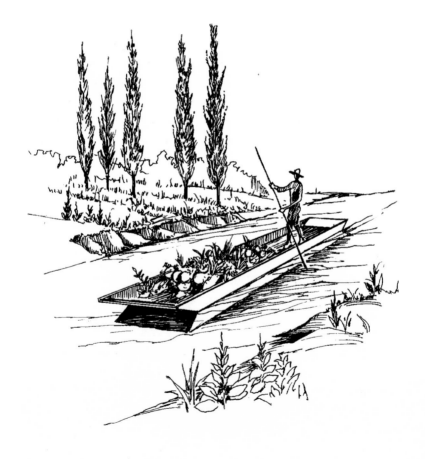

3

Sustainable farming in Aztec times

Prior to European contact in 1519, how did the Aztecs obtain their food? The forerunners of the Aztecs, the Mexica, faced a particular dilemma, largely of their own making. Mexica legend tells how they left their home, Aztlán (believed by many to be the island of Mexcaltitán in Nayarit), on a lengthy pilgrimage lasting hundreds of years. They were seeking a specific sign telling them where to found a new capital and ceremonial center. The sign was an eagle perched on a cactus. Today, this unlikely combination, with the eagle devouring a serpent, is a national symbol and appears on coins and the national flag.

The Mexica's food dilemma arose because they first encountered their sign on an island in the middle of a lake in central Mexico. Here, in 1325, they began to erect their impressive new capital, Tenochtitlan. Building on an island, linked to the lake shoreline via several causeways, might have had some advantages in terms of defense, but supplying the growing settlement with food and fresh water was more of a challenge.

Much of their food came from hunting and gathering, and some food was brought by long-distance trade, but land suitable for farming, especially on the island, was at a premium.

The Mexica/Aztecs solved the dilemma of how to supply food to their island capital by developing a sophisticated wetland farming system involving raised beds, or *chinampas*, built in the lake.

Originally these *chinampas* were free-floating, but over time they became rooted to the lake floor. The *chinampas* were separated by narrow canals, barely wide enough for small boats or canoes. From an ecological perspective, *chinampas* represented an extraordinary achievement: a food production system which proved to be one of the most environmentally sustainable and high-yielding farming systems anywhere on the planet!

Constructing and maintaining *chinampas* required a significant input of labor, but the yields per unit area could be very high indeed, especially since up to four harvests a year were possible for some crops. The system enabled fresh produce to be supplied to the city even during the region's long dry season, whereas food availability from rain-fed agriculture was highly seasonal.

The planting platforms or *chinampas* were built by hand, with alternate layers of mud, silt and vegetation piled onto a mesh of reeds or branches. Platforms, usually rectangular, were about 10 meters wide and could be 100 meters or more in length. Willow trees were often planted on the edges of platforms to help stabilize them and provide shade for other plants and for the canals that separated the platforms. Interplanting crops was common and polyculture was the norm.

Because the planting platforms were close to water, extremes of temperature were ameliorated and the likelihood of frost damage to crops reduced. The root systems of crops had reliable access to fresh water (sub-irrigation). The canals provided a variety of habitats for fish. The mud from the bottom of canals was periodically dredged up by hand and added to the platforms, supplying nutrients and preserving water depth in the canals. Together with the regular addition of waste organic material (compost), this replenished the platforms and meant that their fertility could be maintained over very long periods of time.

The system could even cope with polluted water, since the combination of constant filtration on the platforms and aquatic weeds in the canals partially removed most impurities from the water. Better yet, the blue-green algae spirulina proliferated in the canals. Spirulina proved to be a superfood: a powerful combination of nutrients, including protein, vitamins, minerals, carotenoids and antioxidants. It also had a protein productivity twenty times higher than that of soybeans.

Archaeologists have found vestiges of former *chinampas* in several regions of Mexico, some dating back almost 3000 years, but the easiest *chinampas* to see today are those in Xochimilco on the south-eastern outskirts of Mexico City. Xochimilco is a UNESCO World Heritage site, but faces heavy pressure from urban encroachment and highway construction. Xochimilco's canals, separating the *chinampas*, are some of the last surviving remnants of the large lake that occupied this valley when the Mexica founded Tenochtitlan. Visiting Xochimilco's canals and market is a popular weekend excursion for Mexico City residents and tourists alike.

The modern-day *chinampas* of Xochimilco are not quite the same as they would have been centuries ago. First, the total area of chinampas in Xochimilco is only a fraction of what once existed. Second, some of the chinampas have been abandoned, while on others chemical fertilizers and pesticides are often used. Third, the area now has many exotic species, including introduced species of fish (such as African tilapia and Asian carp) that threaten native species. Numbers of the *axolotl* (a local salamander), a prized delicacy on Aztec dinner tables, are in sharp decline. Fourth, the water table in this area fell dramatically during the 20th century as Mexico City sucked water from the underground aquifers causing local springs that helped supply Xochimilco to dry up completely. In addition, rubble from the cleanup after the 1985 Mexico City earthquake was dumped into Xochimilco's canals.

Historically, lakes in several other parts of Mexico were also used for *chinampa* farming. For example, Magdalena Lake, just west of Guadalajara in Jalisco, was a prime source of food for the 60,000 or so people living close to the Guachimontones ceremonial site near Teuchitlán. The inhabitants of Guachimontones, first settled before 350BC, constructed fixed mud *chinampa* beds in the lake, each measuring about 20 meters by 15 meters, and planted them with various food crops. The remains of hundreds of these highly productive islets are still visible today.

Similar agricultural systems were employed by Indian groups in the coastal marshes along the Gulf coast of Mexico. In the 1980s development experts tried improving rural food production in Tabasco by readopting the Aztec method of building *chinampas* to farm the local wetlands. In the most ambitious, federally-organized project, 65 massive platforms (*camellones*) were built in the Chontalpa swamps. Each platform was 30 meters wide and 100 to 300 meters long. Even though the project was backed by the local Chontal community, the platforms were built by large mechanical dredgers rather than by relying on laborious hand labor.

When the local people began farming the platforms, initial results were very disappointing. Things gradually improved, especially when the Chontal took full control of the project. They shifted the emphasis away from the market-led vegetable production favored by federal officials to growing corn (maize), beans and bananas for local household consumption, improving local food availability. Recent press reports suggest that insufficient investment in maintenance has caused some of the platforms to be abandoned.

This particular project was not without its critics. For example, Mac Chapin of Cultural Survival pointed to fundamental flaws in its planning. One of the most serious problems was that using dredges to construct the platforms had inverted the soil profile, bringing infertile clay to the surface, while sending nutrient-rich layers downwards, beyond the reach of plant roots.

Even if this re-adoption ultimately failed, *chinampa* farming has proven to be one of the greatest ever agricultural advances in the Americas. Among other things, it allowed settlements to thrive in areas where rain, and therefore rain-fed food production, was markedly seasonal. It was, and still can be, an environmentally-sensitive and sustainable method of intensive wetland agriculture.

4

Pyramid sounds and the Maya blues

Modern sound recordings are designed to be as portable and convenient as possible. The Maya people inhabiting the Yucatán Peninsula in south-eastern Mexico had different priorities. Acoustic expert David Lubman has proposed that the earliest sound recording yet discovered on the planet may well be a pyramid: specifically, the main pyramid at Chichen Itza, the archaeological site between Mérida and Cancún.

While we may never know for certain whether the sound effect was truly intentional, the sound can still be heard today by standing in front of the pyramid and making a single hand clap. The resulting echo from the pyramid's stairway is unusual, and sounds like a downward chirp starting from a higher pitch and sliding lower. Lubman makes a strong case for this chirp being a deliberate representation of the call of a local bird, the resplendent quetzal. This bird, labeled "the most spectacular bird in the New World" in Peterson and Chalif's *Field Guide to Mexican Birds*, was formerly common in the rainforest which originally cloaked this region. The beautiful quetzal birds were sacred to the Maya and their colorful feathers were highly prized.

Links between the main pyramid at Chichen Itza—the Pyramid of Kukulkan which rises 25 meters (80 feet) above the ground—and the quetzal bird are supported by the fact that Ku-

kulkan was a Maya deity corresponding to the feathered serpent, more usually known in central Mexico as Quetzalcoatl. Maya depictions of Kukulkan often show the distinctively long feathers typical of the quetzal.

The Maya were masterful astronomers. The Kukulkan pyramid is a precisely-aligned masterpiece, reflecting careful astronomical observations. At each equinox, the sun's rays in the late afternoon create shadows that dance like a slithering snake down the pyramid's steps. It has become customary, especially at the time of the life-affirming Spring equinox in March, for thousands of people to gather in front of the Kukulkan pyramid to greet the appearance of the snake as it wriggles its way down the steps. Most spectators, however, are probably not aware of the pyramid's extraordinary, quetzal-imitating acoustic property.

One of the curiosities about Chichen Itza for many visitors is why the pyramid has such unusually narrow steps with risers between them of such an exaggerated height. Lubman's research may provide an unexpected answer. Previous explanations have resorted to arguments about aesthetics, rather than function. Lubman, however, believes that function is the key, and that the steps were very carefully and deliberately designed in order to maximize the chirped echo effect.

His measurements and calculations suggest that the length of the stairway means that the complete echo lasts more than 100 milliseconds. The reason it sounds like a downward chirp is because the complete echo is actually made up of a whole series of individual echoes, one from each of the 92 steps comprising the sloping staircase. Since the steps are progressively further away from the listener as the sound travels up the stairway, each successive echo is correspondingly delayed fractionally with respect to previous echos, and arrives with a slightly different frequency. The end result is an echo that sounds remarkably like a quetzal bird.

The effect is best heard from relatively close to the pyramid. From three to four meters (10 to 15 feet) in front of the stairway, the chirp is clear. From further back, the difference in frequencies is so small that the effect becomes less obvious.

In 2007 Chichen Itza was designated one of the "New Seven Wonders of the World." The site covers an area of 6.5 square kilometers (2.5 square miles) and has lots of other fascinating sights besides the main pyramid. The astronomical observatory used by the Maya, for example, was a building known as El Caracol ("The Snail") because of its interior spiral staircase. Dating from around AD900, it has features aligned so precisely that they helped the Maya determine the precise dates of many regular celestial happenings, including each of the two annual equinoxes. Evening sound and light shows illustrate the equinoctial serpent effect in dramatic fashion, whatever the time of the year.

The Sacred Cenote (Sacred Sinkhole) at Chichen Itza was used by the ancient Maya for ceremonial purposes, including human sacrifice. The Maya associated the color blue with sacrifice, perhaps because their intent was to placate the rain god and ensure that this arid region received sufficient water for bountiful crops in the coming year. When archaeologists dredged the well, hundreds of valuable artifacts were recovered, but one of the greatest surprises was the discovery of a four-meter-thick layer of blue silt at the bottom of the sinkhole.

Human sacrifices at this site are also thought to be linked to the Temple of the Warriors, where victims were allegedly stripped and then painted blue, prior to having their hearts removed. Remnants of blue coloration are also found on the decorations of many artifacts, such as pottery bowls, and in many murals.

The blue pigment, known as Maya Blue, was first identified in 1931, but precisely how the Maya made it puzzled several generations of archaeologists and chemists. Maya Blue is remarkably stable, retaining its vivid color even in the Yucatán Peninsula's tropical climate. Because of its resistance to acid, weathering processes, biodegradation and even modern chemical solvents, Maya Blue has been hailed by researcher Simon Martin and his colleagues as "one of the great technological and artistic achievements of Mesoamerica".

Early archaeologists supposed that Maya Blue came from copper or lapis lazuli but more recent studies have proved that it was manufactured by a process in which the leaves of the indigo plant were infused into a clay mineral, palygorskite, a type of fuller's earth with medicinal properties. The combination produced Maya Blue's unique chemical bond. In the past decade archaeologists have shown that making Maya Blue was an integral part of the ritual accompanying sacrifices at the Sacred Cenote. It was made on the spot by burning a mixture of copal, indigo and palygorskite. So many sacrificial victims were painted blue and thrown into the sinkhole to placate the rain god that the thick layer of sediment at the bottom acquired its blue tint.

Chichen Itza is one of the most visited archaeological sites in Mexico. To get the most out of your visit, try to stay overnight near the site and arrive before the tour buses, so that you have the opportunity to test the hand clap echo for yourself. When you do, spare a thought for the ancient Maya people who did exactly the same centuries ago. It is quite likely that they too marveled at this curious sound effect.

5

Rubber balls and Americas' oldest ballgame

By far the oldest ballgame in the Americas and the earliest in the world to use a rubber ball is the little known game now known as ulama. Amazingly, this game has been played in some regions of Mexico (its home) for 3500 years.

The original ballgame, played by the Aztecs and other Nahuatl-speaking peoples in Mexico at the time of the Spanish conquest, was known as *ullamaliztli*, a name derived from *ullama* (the playing of a game with a ball) and *ulli* (rubber). Conquistador Hernán Cortés was so impressed with the game that he took two teams of players back to Spain with him in 1528 to show Spanish King Charles I how it was played.

The Spanish court enjoyed watching the demonstration, but was totally stunned by the speed and bounce of the ball, which reacted quite unlike the hair and feather-filled leather balls then in use in Europe. Mexican rubber balls were soon in demand throughout Europe, and became the basis for many of the sports played today.

Despite their initial interest in the game, the Spanish rulers soon decided that ulama was a heathen pastime. They tore down as many ballcourts as they could find in Mexico, and tried to ban the game completely. Fortunately, they were not very successful on either count.

Many archaeological sites in Mexico boast the remains of one or more ballcourts where the game was played, and hundreds of representations of ballgame players are known in pre–Columbian art. Some, dating back as far as 1500BC, depict their characteristic protective gear. The protective padding was necessary because the solid rubber ball used in the game weighed between two and three kilograms (seven to eight pounds) and was propelled at speeds of up to 100 km/h (60 mph).

While most ballgame relics depict single players, one polished clay model found in the state of Nayarit shows a game in progress. Most figurines and carvings depict male players, though a few, even as far back as 800BC, depict female participants.

The precise rules of the ancient game are lost in the mists of antiquity, but the general idea was for the two teams of players to compete at keeping a round rubber ball in motion, without using their hands or feet. Points were gained if the opposing team failed to return the ball or if the ball was driven deep into the opposing end zone. Later ballcourts also included vertical stone rings set high off the ground either side of the I-shaped court, with points awarded whenever the ball was knocked through the ring. These stone "hoops" may well be what inspired Canadian James Naismith to invent basketball in 1891.

The oldest known ballcourt in Mexico is at Paso de la Amada in Chiapas. Rediscovered only a few years ago, it dates back to about 1400BC. Early ballcourts consisted of open areas with two mounds, but later courts were masonry structures that were partially or fully enclosed to create a long, narrow field of play, with perfect viewing opportunities and a more stadium-like atmosphere. Stone rings or hoops were added from around AD900.

Ballcourts varied in size, with the largest one, at the Maya site of Chichen Itza, measuring about 100 meters by 30 meters (315 by 100 feet).

While not all archaeological sites in Mexico have ballcourts, many have more than one. For instance, El Tajín in Veracruz has

18 courts, while nearby Cantona has no fewer than 24. More than 1500 ballcourts are known, from Arizona in the north to Central America in the south.

There are three main variants of modern-day ulama, using the hip, forearm and a heavy, two-handed paddle respectively. Hip ulama players wear a loin cloth (*maxtlatl*) and protective leather hipguards to deflect a ball that can weigh up to three kilos (seven pounds). A lighter ball is used for forearm ulama, which is more akin to volleyball, while paddle ulama, played with a half-kilo ball, looks more like a game of field hockey.

All three variants are still played in western Mexico, with Sinaloa being a hot spot for playing or watching the sport. On the other side of the country, a tourist theme park near Cancún has introduced its own version, which largely ignores the traditional rules and is designed purely as a tourist spectacle.

Ulama had immense significance in pre–Columbian times. The sport was far more than just an athletic contest and had deep religious or mystic symbolism. The *Popul Vuh*, the sacred book of the Maya, describes a ballgame that pits good against evil and revolves around human sacrifice, fertility and regeneration.

The game was a regular part of feast days. It was dangerous, not only on account of injuries resulting from the heavy ball traveling at high speed but also because carved reliefs at some ballcourts, including that at Chichen Itza, suggest that the losing team could, literally, lose their heads.

Post-conquest accounts report that gambling on games was rife, with onlookers prepared to wager their homes, land, corn crops, and allegedly even their children, on the outcome.

Dutch researcher Dr. Ted Leyenaar asserts that the fact that the "Mesoamerican ballgame has survived and flourished for more than 3000 years earns it the distinction of being one of humanity's great cultural expressions." Regrettably, a campaign spearheaded by the Mazatlán Historic Society to have ulama added to UNESCO's World Heritage List in the "Intangible Heritage" category" was not successful. Surely it is time that the Mexican Tourism Secretariat stepped up and revived the campaign, thereby guaranteeing the long-term future of this unusual and ancient sport.

The most enduring long-term legacy of ulama for the rest of the world has been the bouncing rubber ball. But just how did this invention come about? Archaeologists have known for a long time that the pre–Columbian peoples of Mexico made rubber objects, including balls, from the sap or latex of the native Panama rubber tree (*Castilla elastica*). Among the earliest and best-preserved rubber balls are those dating from 1250BC found in waterlogged deposits at El Manati, in Veracruz.

However, barely twenty years ago, it suddenly dawned on Dorothy Hosler, an associate professor of archeology and ancient technology at the Massachusetts Institute of Technology, and two of her colleagues, chemist Sandra Burkett and undergraduate student Michael Tarkanian, that unprocessed pure latex was sticky and became brittle when dry. Put simply, balls made of pure latex did not bounce very well at all, but shattered on impact into many pieces. The trio of scientists set out to tackle the mystery of what makes rubber balls bounce, and eventually worked out the ingenious trick employed by indigenous Mexicans to turn sticky, brittle latex into suitably stretchy elastic material.

Picking up on hints from documentary sources and ethnographic research, Hosler's team decided that Mexico's indigenous Indians had probably mixed natural latex with the juice of the morning glory vine, moonflower (*Ipomoea alba*). This plant, prized for its curative properties, has impressive, fragrant, alabaster-colored flowers that form fluted funnels up to 15 centimeters (6 inches) in diameter. The researchers carefully squeezed some moonflower juice into a bucket containing latex and stirred for fifteen minutes. The liquid latex solidified into a white mass, pliable enough to be formed by hand into a ball. The researchers shaped a ball about 9.5 centimeters (3.7 inches) in diameter and, lo and behold, it bounced! After using nuclear magnetic resonance scans to examine rubber balls dating from 1600BC found in Veracruz and Chiapas, they concluded that these must have been made in a very similar fashion.

The addition of sap to the latex began complex chemical changes that provided a flexible material much better suited for tools, figurines and medicines. This was effectively an early version of the vulcanization process invented three thousand years later by Charles Goodrich. Adding sap to otherwise brittle rubber had inadvertently created the perfect rubber balls for the development of ulama.

We should not be surprised that pre–Columbian Indians discovered this chemical trick thousands of years ago, since tropical botanists know that the two plants, *Castilla elastica* and *Ipomoea alba,* are often found in close proximity. In fact, moonflower vines often twine themselves around rubber trees, making it quite likely that the first bouncy rubber was the direct result of a careless rubber tapper accidentally contaminating the latex he was collecting with a little moonflower: a happy accident that turned out to have incredibly serendipitous results, not just for Mexico, but for many of the world's major sports to this day.

6

Roman symbols on a Maya pyramid?

I've always tried to maintain an open mind about history, but even I was incredulous when I first heard of the possible links between a pyramid in Tabasco and the Romans. This is certainly not an idea you will find in most history books, but could it possibly be true?

The evidence comes from Comalcalco, an archaeological site on the swampy Gulf coastal plain of Tabasco in southeastern Mexico. The name Comalcalco derives from "in the house of the comals", comals being the flat griddles used (even today) to cook tortillas. Comalcalco's first inhabitants were the Olmec, sometimes referred to as Mexico's "mother culture", who flourished from 1500–400BC. They built Mexico's very first pyramid, modeled after the slopes of a local volcano, at La Venta, only 80 kilometers (50 miles) west of Comalcalco.

The Olmec eventually abandoned Comalcalco, but centuries later the site was reoccupied, this time by the Chontal group of Maya. The site is small, but has 375 distinct structures, including a large, stepped pyramid. It is the westernmost Maya site known to archaeologists. Only when you take a close look at the walls, does it become apparent how different this site is to other Maya sites. Instead of the carefully-hewn blocks of limestone normally employed by the Maya, Comalcalco's pyramids are built of thousands and thousands of flat, rectangular bricks.

The local Chontal Maya had no easy access to limestone (by far the commonest rock on the Yucatán Peninsula further east), so they adopted an entirely different strategy when building. They learned to shape and fire the local clay into *tabiques* (fired bricks). Almost all of Comalcalco's many constructions are built of these *tabiques*, held in place by a mortar made mainly from oyster shells.

I first visited Comalcalco only because I wanted to see just what a brick-built pyramid looked like. I found the workmanship impressive and marveled at the organization required to build such a site. Several years elapsed before I learned that Comalcalco held another massive secret, one than still makes me yearn for a return visit.

Archaeologists restoring the site discovered that many of the bricks had inscriptions marked on them. Where the bricks were still firmly set in mortar, the inscriptions were completely hidden from view. Bricks that had been dislodged, and those removed for repointing during restoration, often bore mysterious symbols or inscriptions. In rare cases, even the brick makers' fingerprints were still clearly visible.

Neil Steede, one of the archaeologists working at the site, studied 4612 of these bricks (weighing 21 tons), and photographed the inscriptions found on about 1500 of them. Most of the symbols or inscriptions have been interpreted as being brick masons' signs. The really curious thing about Comalcalco is that these marks turn out to be virtually identical to the masons' marks used by the Romans, half a world away. Steede came to the astonishing conclusion that the "illustrated bricks" were "pieces to a grand puzzle", which on completion "may reveal a Roman Christian presence in the Americas a thousand years before the arrival of Columbus."

The inscriptions on the bricks are not the only evidence for early European contact at this site. Other researchers claim that the exact dimensions and proportions of the bricks (more like tablets than conventional house bricks), and some of the architectural details, are more Roman than Maya.

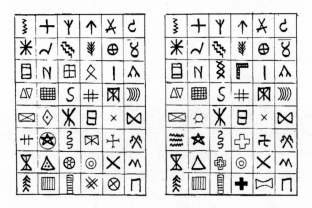

Similarities of masons' marks from Roman sites (left) and Comalcalco (right). Figure 10 in Fell (1990), reproduced by kind permission of Dr. Julian Fell and the Epigraphic Society.

The image shows some typical mason's signs found on Roman bricks (left) and Comalcalco bricks (right). Many additional similarities exist between masons' signs found on bricks from Comalcalco and those from Roman, Minoan, and ancient Greek sites. The similarities are truly amazing!

No one is suggesting that the Roman Empire stretched across the Atlantic, but is it actually possible that Romans once set foot on what is now Mexican soil? Proponents of early transatlantic contacts believe that the Roman influences were introduced by Indian contacts with the New World. Specifically, they argue that the Indian Satavahana Dynasty (200BC to AD200) had developed extensive trade connections with Rome, and that their own Brahmi script soon reached Comalcalco. The technology used to make kiln-fired bricks at Comalcalco was very similar to that used in parts of South East Asia. In addition, the urn-burials found at Comalcalco appear to be virtually contemporaneous with similar burials in India.

Many, though not all, of the inscriptions chiseled into bricks at Comalcalco can be interpreted. Clyde Winters and Neil Steede examined the iconography of the symbols in some detail. Winters, an expert on Olmec script, which predated the rise of the Maya, quickly recognized that one particular brick (T1-452 R16) was the local equivalent of the Rosetta Stone, having both Olmec and Maya scripts, side by side. Steede interpreted the Maya side, while Winters interpreted the Olmec script of this brick. When they compared notes, they found that the left side in Maya was essentially a translation of the right side in Olmec; the brick was bilingual.

After examining many more bricks from the site, Winters came to believe that Comalcalco was possibly the Maya equivalent of a trade school, where scribes learned Maya writing and translated Olmec glyphs, tabique-makers perfected their craft, and construction crews worked on their building techniques. Bricks with inscriptions are not randomly located within the structures. Steede has documented how those depicting plants and animals are found in the lower sections of walls, those depicting people in the upper sections, and those with geometric or numeric signs in the ceiling structures.

Evidence from the inscribed bricks shows that when the site was at its peak, during Classic times, it was a close ally of, perhaps controlled by, the powerful Maya leader Pakal and his successors residing at Palenque. Artifacts found at Comalcalco suggest links to Maya sites as far away as Tikal in Guatemala.

The site today does not look the same as it did in Maya times. It would have been far more colorful then. The Chontal Maya covered the exterior surfaces of all the bricks with stucco—remnants of which are still visible in some places—and they often carved ornate reliefs into the stucco for further decoration.

I have no idea whether or not transoceanic settlers helped build Comalcalco but this particular archaeological site has me enthralled. Its bricks may still conceal far more stories than we ever thought possible. The secrets of its master masons may yet emerge!

The archaeological site is about three kilometers outside the small town of Comalcalco, a lively farming center with few tourist services. The nearest large city, Villahermosa, is 60 kilometers (45 miles) to the south-east. At the archaeological site, the small site museum should not be missed. It displays a pair of water pipes unique to Comalcalco, as well as carved figurines and heads that portray features such as beards and hats, neither of which are commonly associated with Maya iconography.

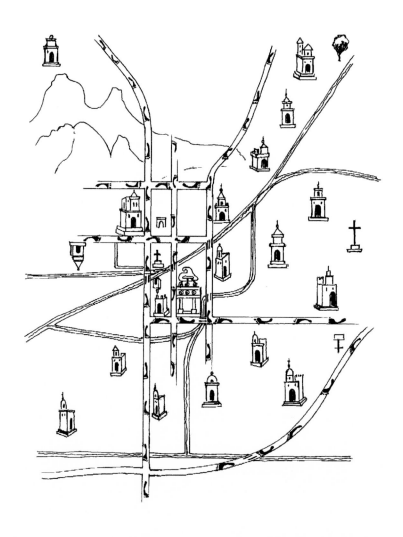

Spanish rule (New Spain)

7

Post-conquest inventory

Throughout history, most conquerors have had only imperfect knowledge of precisely how much territory and wealth they have gained until after the last battle was won and victory was assured. Once celebrations were over, they needed to take stock of what they had acquired.

In many cases, one of their first post-conquest steps, therefore, was to undertake a comprehensive survey of everything of value, or potential value. For example, in England, after the Norman Conquest of 1066, William the Conqueror ordered a detailed survey of his newly acquired territories. The results of the survey were compiled to form the Domesday Book. The decision to send out assessors to every corner of the land was made because William wanted to know "what or how much each landholder had, in land or livestock, and how much money it was worth", so that he could tax it accordingly.

On the other side of the Atlantic, the Aztecs had also expanded through conquests, gradually establishing an empire that stretched from the Gulf coast to the Pacific. They too kept records of their spoils, though these were more pictorial and far less wordy than the Domesday Book. In order to administer the tributes due from every part of their empire, they recorded the requisite payments of everything, from feathers and live animals to minerals and food, on bark paper codices. Only a few of these documents survived the Spanish conquest. Many of those that did were subsequently destroyed by narrow-minded and overeager conquistadors and priests.

Fortunately, a handful of more enlightened priests recognized the vast store of knowledge portrayed by indigenous codices and encouraged early converts to share their knowledge by making new, illustrated bark paper rolls. The Codex Mendoza, one of several post–conquest codices, recorded many aspects of Aztec life, including the tributes payable by the various villages and towns.

For example, one page in the Codex Mendoza shows that the tribute for a single village included the following:

    2 strings of beads of jadeite, a green semiprecious stone
    160 skins of the bird with blue plumage
    4000 handfuls of colored feathers
    2 brick-sized slabs of clear amber
    2 labrets (lip piercings) of amber encased in gold
    40 jaguar skins
    200 loads of cacao beans, the main ingredient of chocolate
    800 tecomates (cups for drinking chocolate)

Such tribute lists held little interest to the Spaniards when they arrived, since some of the items held in high esteem by the Aztecs were deemed worthless by the conquerors. Conversely, other goods which were of little or no consequence to the Aztecs, such as silver, were highly prized in Europe.

After the conquest, the Spanish Court was determined to acquire accurate information about everything being encountered in New Spain. This required a series of censuses and accounts, the most comprehensive of which were the *Geographic Accounts* (*Relaciones geográficas*), which began in the late 16th century.

Shortly after being named Visitor of the Council of the Indies in 1569, Juan de Ovando y Godoy sent a survey containing 37 questions to the New World. Another questionnaire, with about 200 questions, was issued in 1570. A few years later, perhaps in an effort to elicit more responses from the provinces, Ovando y Godoy's successor, Juan López de Velasco, reduced the number of questions to 50. These 50 questions, sent to New Spain in 1577, became the basis for the *Geographic Accounts*, an inventory that was Spain's equivalent of the Domesday Book.

The authorities in each administrative center were instructed to hold a meeting of the "Spaniards and other natives" in each district, to find out everything they could about the area's people, geography and history.

Of the 191 known responses to this 1577 questionnaire, 167 have survived to the present day. Most of the original responses are housed in Spain, in either the Archivo General de las Indias in Seville or in the Real Academia de la Historia in Madrid. A further 43 responses reside in the Benson Latin American Collection of the University of Texas at Austin. That library's web page about the *Geographic Accounts* has links to images of sample pages and maps.

The style and substance of a typical account can be judged by these extracts of the response in 1579 from Xiquilpan [Jiquilpan] in Michoacán. Today, Jiquilpan is a mid-sized town west of Zamora, a short distance from the southern shore of Lake Chapala. The town library has stark murals painted by José Clemente Orozco and an entrance door with magnificent bronze sculpting.

But what was Jiquilpan like in 1579?

"Xiquilpan is in temperate land.... A river, which never dries up, flows through the village. It carries very little water in summer, but in winter often rises so high that it cannot be crossed. Less than one league from this village toward the north is a lake called Chapala, which is forty leagues around. A lot of white fish and catfish, and another kind of small fish, are caught in it". [Note that one league was the distance that could be walked in an hour, so varied from four to seven kilometers (two and a half to four miles), depending on the terrain.]

"Xilquilpan has ... about a hundred tributary Indians. They say that before the land was won, there were 1200 people. Since the lands were won, their number has diminished as a result of the many diseases that have occurred. In particular, in 1576, there was a great plague in this village, common throughout New Spain, which led to the deaths of a large number of people."

"There is a wild plant in this village which cures those who are crippled. It has leaves like a lettuce and is so hot that the part where the root is put burns naturally, like a fire. There is another plant, a root similar to *camote*, which is a preventive for everything. They cure with these herbs and with others that the natives know."

"In this village, and its surrounding area, grow pears, figs, pomegranates, grapes, peaches, quinces, nuts and apples, all Castilian [Spanish] fruits. Native [plants] include avocados, sweet canes, guavas, *capulines* (which are local cherries), squash, chile, tomatoes and a lot of corn. They grow cabbages, lettuce, onions, radishes, blites, and every kind of vegetable from Spain. Wheat and barley grow in this village."

"The main animals found in the village are wolves, which breed in the swamps that surround some reed beds. More than eighty thousand sheep come from other parts to pasture seasonally on the edge of this village each year."

"There are no salt beds in this village; the natives supply themselves with salt from Colima, twenty leagues from this village, and from the province called Avalos fifteen leagues away".

These *Geographic Accounts* are of immense value in reconstructing the past history of Mexico. The detail in them is often quite astonishing. However, as historian René Acuña has emphasized, while the *Geographic Accounts* provide invaluable information about local cultures, they should never be considered completely reliable. They were not eyewitness accounts, but relied on hearsay and on the possibly dubious interpretations made by a relatively small number of respondents.

8

Oldest winery in the Americas

In Mexico, vineyards and wineries exist in several states, including Baja California, Sonora, Zacatecas, Querétaro and Coahuila. Wine experts usually claim that Mexico's finest wines come from Baja California, but award-winning wines are also now emerging from Casa Madero, the oldest winery anywhere in the Americas. Casa Madero, formally established as long ago as 1597, is located in Parras de la Fuente, a small town in the northern state of Coahuila.

In 1549 the Spanish priests and soldiers who explored this region discovered native vines growing wild in a valley and chose the spot to found the Mission of Santa María de Las Parras ("Holy Mary of the Vines"). The early Mission of Santa María soon began to make wine from the local grapes, and a few years later the wines and brandies of the Valley of Parras were being shipped to the rest of the Americas.

The valley's natural conditions proved to be ideal for viticulture. At 1500 meters (5000 feet) above sea level, this region enjoys warm days and cool nights, and is richly endowed with an ample supply of water from natural springs, supplemented nowadays by water obtained from deep wells. The name Parras de la Fuente (literally "grapevines of the fountain") is in honor of Antonio de la Fuente, a 19th century politician.

The area's earliest vineyard was planted in 1593 by Francisco de Urdiñola at El Rosario Hacienda, an estate that gained fame much later as the birthplace of Mexican revolutionary hero Francisco I. Madero in 1873. Ignobly, that hacienda has long since been transformed into a shopping center.

A photograph in the August 1996 *National Geographic* shows grapes at the Marqués de Aguayo winery in Parras being crushed underfoot in 1922 by workers moving in time to a harpist, because "pressing grapes by machinery sometimes breaks up the seeds, which give an unpleasant taste." Today, a modern French machine does the job, without any coffee breaks, timeouts, or unpleasant taste. The Marqués de Aguayo winery could once claim to be the oldest in the Americas, but, after it closed in 1989, the title passed to its present incumbent, the Madero vineyard.

Casa Madero, as it is now known, was originally founded on 19 August 1597 at the San Lorenzo hacienda, land granted by King Philip II of Spain to Lorenzo García. The town of Parras was officially founded the following year.

The fame of the town's wines spread quickly, but in 1699 Spain's King Charles II banned all production of wine in the New World except by or for the church. The ban, issued to protect Spanish winemakers, lasted for more than a century. The San Lorenzo vineyard continued to supply the local Franciscan Mission before being purchased in 1893 by Francisco I. Madero's grandfather, Evaristo Madero, who soon introduced European vines and techniques.

José Milmo, the present owner of the beautifully-restored San Lorenzo hacienda, is a great grandson of Evaristo Madero, and has focused on growing premium grapes for table wines, especially varieties suitable for Chardonnay, Merlot, Shiraz and Cabernet Sauvignon. Milmo has also introduced modern and high-tech cultivation methods, ranging from underground drip irrigation to nighttime harvesting. All of Casa Madero's wines (which are mainly reds) come from 1000 acres of estate-grown grapes; the winery produces about 320,000 cases a year, many of them exported to the U.S., Europe and Japan.

Casa Grande Shiraz, one of Madero's premium wines, won a gold medal at an International Wine Competition in Brussels, Belgium, in 2003. The vintner's Chenin Blanc 2012 gained top prize as the world's best dry white wine in the prestigious 2013 Vinalies Internationales Competition in Paris, France, beating more than 3400 other wines from 43 countries in the process. This is the single highest award ever won by a Mexican wine.

The town of Parras de la Fuente, designated by Mexico's Tourism Secretariat a Magic Town (*Pueblo Mágico*) in 2004, has several old buildings worthy of note. These include the 17th-century church and college of San Ignacio de Loyola, where the stone fountain is decorated with sculpted grapes, and the Santuario de Nuestra Señora de Guadalupe.

As you wander the town's cobblestone streets, look for the grapevines painted around some older doorways. Old-time movie buffs will get a sense of déjà vu in some parts of town, as this is where the classic western *The Wild Bunch* (1969) was filmed. The ruins of the nearby Hacienda Ciénega del Carmen also featured in some scenes.

Overlooking the town of Parras is the simple 19th-century Santo Madero Chapel, rising atop the plug of an extinct volcano. From here, stunning views extend over the town, vineyards, farms and neighboring mountains. On account of its springs, vineyards and orchards of pecan trees, Parras de la Fuente is considered the "oasis of Coahuila".

In addition to Casa Madero, Parras has several smaller wineries, catering mainly to the local market. The town's major festival is its lively, annual, week-long Grape Fair, held in early August.

Visitors are welcomed at the Casa Madero winery and its small museum, located eight kilometers (five miles) north of the town. Tours and overnight stays are available and a wine-tasting room is open during business hours. When touring the winery, look for the tiled mural of the Virgin of Wine, which adds a whole new dimension to the saying "a night on the tiles".

Parras de la Fuente is in the state of Coahuila, about 180 kilometers (110 miles) west of Monterrey, midway between the cities of Saltillo and Torreón. The town offers a full range of tourist services. While Casa Madero offers deluxe accommodations, families with children may prefer the expansive Hotel Rincón del Montero resort, a short distance out of town.

9

Baaad sheep depleted environment

As we saw in chapters 1 and 3, Mexico's indigenous inhabitants had a rich and varied diet based on the large number of food crops that are native to Mexico, supplemented by animals they bred, caught or hunted. Before the Spanish arrived, there were very few domesticated animals in Mexico, the main exceptions being dogs, rabbits and turkeys.

Early Spanish settlers introduced numerous Old World species to the New World. Some were deliberately introduced, some accidentally; some proved to be valuable additions, others turned out to be disastrous.

Estimates for the number of people living in Mexico before Europeans arrived range from 4 million to 30 million. Hernán Cortés and his band of conquistadors arrived in Mexico in 1519 and defeated the Aztecs, taking control of their capital city Tenochtitlan in 1521.

The spread of Spanish colonial rule and administration during the remainder of the 16th century had unexpected and calamitous social impacts on the indigenous societies. The indigenous population was decimated during the century following the arrival of Spaniards and crashed to about 1.6 million, mostly as a result of smallpox and other European diseases such as measles, influenza, typhus and bubonic plague. Mexico's population dropped by between 75 and 90 percent, one of the most dramatic population declines in human history.

While the most pernicious accidental introductions, beyond any doubt, were human-borne diseases, the Spaniards also brought noxious weeds and rodents. Many of the respondents whose testimonies formed the 16th century *Geographic Accounts* (chapter 7) recognized both the dramatic impact of imported diseases on population numbers and the changes wrought by the introduction of Spanish crops, animals and agricultural techniques.

Most plant and animal introductions from Europe were deliberate, brought with the intention of increasing the diversity of available food and resources. Exotic plants that were introduced included wheat, barley, figs, grapes, olives, peaches, quinces, pomegranates, bananas, cabbages, lettuces and radishes, as well as many flowers. Ships from Europe also brought many animals—sheep, pigs, cows, chickens and goats—to ensure that the transplanted Spanish clerics setting up early missions need not lack any home comforts.

The introduction of sheep is a perfect example of how a well-meaning addition to the native fauna led, first, to boom times, but ultimately resulted in disastrous consequences for Mexico's natural environment.

In the Old World, wool had been a major item of trade in Spain for several centuries before the New World was settled. The first conquistadors were quick to recognize the potential that the newly-won territories held for large-scale sheep farming.

The development of sheep farming and its consequences in one area of central Mexico—the Valle de Mezquital in the state of Hidalgo—are analyzed in some detail by Elinor Melville in *A plague of Sheep. Environmental consequences of the Conquest of Mexico*. She argues that the introduction of sheep placed great pressure on the land. Their numbers rose rapidly, but then crashed as overgrazing changed the local environmental conditions.

Melville divides the development of sheep farming in the Valle de Mezquital into several distinct phases. Sheep farming was established in the area by 1530. When the Spaniards first settled the area and saw that Indians did not own any grazing animals or fence their fields, they assumed that the area was considered common land and therefore available for pasturing animals.

Sheep farming took off during Phase I (Expansion, 1530–1565). During this phase, the growth in numbers of sheep in the region was so rapid that the enlightened Spanish Viceroy, Luis de Velasco, took steps to prevent sheep herding from threatening Indian land rights and food production. Velasco recognized the importance to long-term food production of maintaining the strong existing peasant base. Among the regulations introduced to control sheep farming was a ban on letting animals graze within close proximity of any Indian village.

The Viceroy also encouraged the Spanish practice of *agostadero*, a form of seasonal grazing whose name derives from *agosto*, or August. In Spain, *agostadero* meant summer grazing on harvested fields or temporary pastures; in New Spain, it was adopted for dry season grazing, and originally limited to the first two months of each year.

During Phase II (Consolidation of Pastoralism, 1565–1580), the area used for sheep grazing remained fairly stable, but the numbers of sheep, and therefore their grazing density, continued to increase.

By the mid–1570s sheep dominated the regional landscape, and the local Indian people also had flocks. One of the consequences of this was serious environmental degradation. This reached the point where, by the late 1570s, some farmers did not have adequate year-round access to pastures. The duration of the seasonal *agostadero* was lengthened, and many farmers began to move their flocks (some numbering tens of thousands of sheep) more than 160 kilometers (100 miles) during the dry season from their home farms in central Mexico to pastures near Lake Chapala.

This annual movement of sheep had become so important by 1574 that a provision was made for the opening of special sheep lanes or *cañadas* along the route, notwithstanding the considerable environmental damage done by the large migrating flocks. By 1589, at the peak of the sheep bonanza, more than 200,000 animals were involved in the seasonal migration.

By the end of Phase III (The Final Takeover, 1580–1600), most farmland had been incorporated into the Spanish land tenure system, the Indian population had declined (mainly due to disease), and the sheep population had also dropped dramatically. Spanish accounts from that time reveal that the collapse in sheep numbers was attributed to a combination of the killing of too many animals for just their hides by Spaniards, an excessive consumption of lamb and mutton by Indians, and the depletion of flocks by thieves and wild dogs. Melville's research, however, suggested that the main reason for the decline was actually environmental degradation, a direct consequence of the excessive numbers of sheep being raised at an earlier time. In economic terms, it illustrated the tragedy of the commons.

The introduction of sheep had begun well and showed early promise. Sheep numbers had risen rapidly, but then crashed as they imposed irrevocable pressure on the land, far exceeding its carrying capacity. As overgrazing took its toll, the carrying capacity was reduced and the local environmental conditions were permanently changed.

By the 1620s sheep numbers in the Valle de Mezquital had collapsed and would never fully recover. The landscape had been changed forever. During the 18th century in this region, the emphasis shifted from pastoral to arable farming.

10

Afro-Mexicans outnumbered Spaniards

Modern research, using DNA analysis, indicates that Mexican *mestizos* are genetically about one-eighth African. The available evidence suggests that in Mexico the races have melted more than in any other country. While there are relatively few black faces in Mexico, there are isolated pockets of Afro-Mexicans, most notably in Veracruz and on the coast of Guerrero, where aspects of African heritage live on in art, music, dance, food, and even in fishing and agricultural practices.

By common consent, the history of blacks in Mexico is a long one. The first black slave to arrive in Mexico is thought to have been Juan Cortés. He accompanied the conquistadors in 1519. It has been claimed that some natives thought he must be a god, since they had never seen a black man before.

A few years later, six blacks are believed to have taken part in the successful siege of the Aztec capital Tenochtitlan. Several hundred other blacks formed part of the itinerant fighting forces employed in the name of the Spanish crown to secure other parts of New Spain.

New Spain had been conquered by a ludicrously small number of Spaniards. To retain control and in order to begin exploiting the potential riches of the virgin territory they had won, a good supply of laborers was essential. On account of the population

crash resulting from imported diseases (chapter 9), there were too few locals available, so imports of slaves became a high priority.

By 1570 almost 35 percent of all the mine workers in the largest mines of Zacatecas and neighboring locations were African slaves. Large numbers of slaves were also imported for the sugar plantations and factories in areas such as Veracruz on the Gulf coast. By the mid-17th century, some 8000-10,000 blacks were Gulf coast residents. After this time, the slave trade to Mexico gradually diminished.

Miguel Hidalgo, the independence leader, first demanded an end to slavery in 1810, coincidentally the same year that Upper Canada freed all its slaves. Slavery in Mexico was abolished by President Vicente Guerrero on 15 September 1829.

In 1831, recognizing the potential attraction of Mexico for slaves from north of the border, one Mexican senator, Sánchez de Tagle, a signatory of the Act of Independence (*Acta de Independencia*), called for assistance to be given to any blacks who wanted to move south. He argued that supporting this flow of black migrants could possibly prevent Mexico from being invaded by white Americans. During the succeeding years, prior to the abolition of slavery in the U.S. in 1865, many U.S. slaves did indeed seize the chance to escape and headed to Mexico in search of freedom and opportunity.

Sánchez de Tagle's point was that black immigrants would be strong supporters of Mexico since they wouldn't want to be returned into slavery, and would certainly be preferable to white Americans, who might be seeking an opportunity to annex parts of Mexico for their homeland. As we now know, Sánchez de Tagle's fears about U.S. expansionism came to pass. Barely a year after the U.S. annexed the slave-holding Republic of Texas in 1845, it invaded Mexico.

About 4000 blacks are thought to have entered Mexico between 1840 and 1860. At the beginning of 1850, several states enacted a series of land concessions for black immigrants so that undeveloped areas with agricultural potential might be settled and farmed.

Even after the abolition of slavery in the U.S., small waves of blacks continued to arrive periodically in Mexico. Many came from the Caribbean after 1870 to help build the growing national railroad network. In 1882 some 300 Jamaicans arrived to help build the San Luis Potosí-Tampico line; another 300 Jamaicans made the trip in 1905 to take jobs in mines in the state of Durango. Partially in response to their own independence struggles, thousands of Cubans arrived after 1895. They favored the tropical coastal lowlands, such as Veracruz, Yucatán and parts of Oaxaca, where the climate and landscapes were more familiar to them than the conditions on the high interior plateaux of central Mexico.

For a variety of reasons, Mexican historians have tended to ignore the in-migration of blacks and their gradual intermarriage and assimilation into Mexican society, choosing to focus instead on either the indigenous peoples or the mixed race *mestizos* who form the majority of Mexicans today. The pendulum is finally swinging back, led by researchers like Charles Henry Rowell, Ben Vinson III and Bobby Vaughn, who have re-evaluated original sources and examined the life and culture of the communities where many Afro-Mexicans live.

Much of the academic work about the influence of blacks on modern-day Mexico has focused on the Veracruz area, in particular on the settlements of Coyolillo, Alvarado, Mandinga and Tlacotalpan. On the opposite coast, Bobby Vaughn spent more than a decade studying the Costa Chica of Oaxaca and Guerrero.

Analysts of Mexican population history emphasize the poor reliability of early estimates and censuses, as well as the complex mixing of races which occurred with time. While the precise figures and dates may vary, most demographers appear to agree with Bobby Vaughn that the Afro-Mexican population, which rose rapidly to around 20,000 in the mid-16th century, continued to exceed the Spanish population in New Spain until around 1810.

It is estimated that more than 110,000 black slaves (perhaps even as many as 200,000) were brought to New Spain during colonial times. Their legacy is still with us, and lives on in the language, customs and culture of all these areas.

One especially significant musical introduction from the mid–16th century was the knowledge of making xylophones. As early as 1545, a Spanish scribe in the state of Chiapas wrote of an instrument of eight wood bars played with heavy sticks by the local natives at tribal ceremonies. The first marimbas, as they became known, were made by imported slaves familiar with constructing African xylophones. A later innovation in the 19th century saw the addition of a second row of semitone bars to the common single row. This expanded the musical scope of the marimba, allowing it to become the versatile instrument we know and love today.

A modern concert marimba can be three meters long, have 70 keys and weigh more than 55 kilos (110 pounds). The largest marimbas require four musicians, responsible for bass, harmonics, melody and counterpoint or treble, respectively.

African influence on music extends to the popular Mexican folk song "La Bamba", which was popularized by Richie Valens and other performers. While the modern version of "La Bamba" originated in Veracruz, its origins go back to the Bamba district of Angola.

11

Epic journeys and mythical cities

El Fuerte, a small town in the northern state of Sinaloa, played a pivotal role in the history of Mexico's north-west. It was the point of departure for some epic journeys by adventurers in search of legendary cities and gold, and the end-point of one of the most extraordinary transcontinental crossings ever.

El Fuerte became important at a time when Mexico had a much larger land area than today. After independence in 1821, the nation's northern border reached deep into the modern-day U.S. states of Texas, New Mexico, Arizona, California, Utah and Colorado. For three years in the mid–19th century, El Fuerte was the capital of the Western State, an area comprising the present-day states of Sinaloa, Sonora and much of Arizona.

The town developed exceptionally close ties to California and Arizona. Every one of the expeditions to colonize those areas passed through El Fuerte. In the 1848 California gold rush so many of the prospectors seeking their fortune started from El Fuerte that the town suffered a dramatic drop in population. Fortunately, the rush north for gold was offset by the economic opportunities resulting from mineral discoveries closer to home, such as those in the Copper Canyon region.

By the time it was made capital of the Western State, El Fuerte was already more than two hundred years old. Relatively little is

known about the early Indian peoples living in the surrounding
Fuerte Valley, but they probably survived by harvesting wild plants,
farming small gardens, fishing and hunting. They appear to have
had few links with other tribes outside the region.

In 1530 an exploratory group of Spaniards, led by Nuño Beltran de Guzmán (the founder of Guadalajara), had reached the
coastal area near Mazatlán but had not ventured much further
north. Beltran de Guzmán organized follow-up expeditions, and
the first white man to set foot on the shores of the El Fuerte river
(then known as the Zuaque) is thought to have been his nephew,
Diego de Guzmán, in September 1533. The river was so full at
that time that Diego was unable to cross it and continue any
further north.

Meanwhile, Beltran de Guzmán was not the only conquistador
coveting territory in the northern sections of New Spain. Hernán
Cortés himself sent a ship northwards in 1532, in an effort to leap-
frog Beltran de Guzmán and extend his dominions beyond those
already explored by Guzmán. This ship was wrecked in a storm
off the coast near Mazatlán and the entire crew killed by Indians.

Just four years later, in 1536, a truly remarkable meeting, one
of the most astonishing encounters ever, took place just 20 kilometers from El Fuerte. Four Spaniards from El Fuerte were out
riding when they came across four bedraggled individuals who
were thrilled to see them.

It turned out that the four individuals—three Spaniards,
Alvaro Nuñez Cabeza de Vaca, Alonso del Castillo Maldonado,
and Andrés Dorantes de Carranza, and a black slave named Estebanico—were the only survivors of a maritime expedition that set
sail from Cuba in 1518 and had been shipwrecked off the coast of
Florida. It had taken them eighteen years to walk through what
today are the states of Alabama, Louisiana, Texas, New Mexico,
Chihuahua, Sonora and Sinaloa! Their trek, full of adventures and
narrow escapes, is surely one of the most amazing journeys ever
undertaken even to this day. After this astounding transcontinen-

tal peregrination, they stumbled across a Yaqui Indian in Sonora who had the clasp of a sword etched on his collar. Realizing that this meant fellow countrymen must be close, they hurried south and met the four Spaniards on horseback, near what is today the Los Ojitos ranch.

Initial greetings over and their story told, Cabeza de Vaca shared the rumors they had heard, from Indians along the way, of Cíbola, a large province to the north said to have seven walled cities with large houses and lots of gold and silver. Another rich kingdom, Quivira, was supposed to lie in the same general direction.

The first organized attempt to find Cíbola was made by Fray Marcos de Niza, with Estebanico as guide. Reaching Arizona and the lands of the Pueblo Indians, Estebanico was killed. Unwilling to admit defeat, Marcos de Niza returned with exaggerated tales of what he had seen and heard. In 1540 a second expedition was organized, this time led by the redoubtable Francisco Vázquez de Coronado. Coronado's expedition, with 250 horsemen, 60 soldiers and 1000 Indians, traveled a long way north, finding the Grand Canyon (Pedro de Tovar being credited with its "discovery"), and eventually reached the 40th parallel and the Arkansas river. Finding nothing that matched the lyrical descriptions of Cíbola or Quivira, Coronado returned to the Viceroy in 1542. The Seven Cities of Gold became yet another of the many fabulous myths associated with the Spanish quest for New World riches.

Meanwhile, back in the Fuerte Valley, Spanish settlers had founded San Juan de Carapoa in 1564; shortly afterwards it was destroyed by local Mayo Indians. A Jesuit mission, established here in 1590, was subject to repeated Indian uprisings. The martyrdom of a Jesuit priest named Gonzalo de Tapía led to the construction of a rectangular, adobe-walled fort (hence the town's new name of El Fuerte), completed between 1608 and 1610 by Captain Diego Martínez de Hurdaide. The fort, roughly 100 meters by 100 meters in size, and criticized at the time as being far too expensive, became a frontier post, controlling the routes into the surrounding Indian territory. The town subsequently became a trading post for gold and silver and, for almost three centuries, was the most important commercial center of the vast frontier area of north-western Mexico.

Even as El Fuerte grew in importance, Indian conflicts smouldered on, lasting into the first half of the 20th century.

From 1824 to 1826 the riverside town of El Fuerte was the capital of the Western State, the interim state of Sinaloa-Sonora which included part of Arizona and stretched as far north as the Grand Canyon. In 1826 the capital was changed first to Alamos and then to Copala. In 1830 the Western State was divided creating two new states: Sonora and Sinaloa.

Arizona and California remained part of Mexico until after the disastrous 1846–48 U.S. War with Mexico. At the war's conclusion, the 1848 Treaty of Guadalupe Hidalgo ceded over half of Mexico's territory to the U.S. A few years later, the 1853 Gadsden Purchase (Treaty of La Mesilla), also transferred the northern portions of Sonora and Chihuahua to the U.S., thereby establishing the current border between the two countries.

While nothing is left of its original fort, the town of El Fuerte today has a pleasant, partially restored center with typical provincial colonial-style buildings. The town (population about 30,000; elevation about 190 meters) is proud of its traditional Sinaloan culture. Brass and drum bands play *tamboras sinaloenses*, a German-Mexican musical blend peculiar to Sinaloa. Evening activities focus on the shady plaza.

Just off the main plaza, on the slopes of the hill which originally housed the fort, construction began in 1903 of the Almada mansion, now the Posada Hidalgo hotel. Rafael Almada, who later became the Mayor of El Fuerte, was born in Alamos in 1861 and married his cousin, Rafaela, in 1897. Two years later, they moved to El Fuerte and set up a trading business. In the style of the times, whenever Rafaela went to church, she insisted on being taken the block and a half in her four-wheeled carriage (*calash*) rather than walking! The Almadas spent five years and 100,000 gold pesos on constructing their mansion. Sadly, Rafael died suddenly barely two years after its completion; his funeral carriage can still be seen in the hotel. The wooden trim for the building, its 285 pine beams and most of its lavish antique furnishings were brought by boat from San Francisco and unloaded at Topolobampo during the time of Albert K. Owen's utopian colony (chapter 16); ironwork was brought from Mazatlán. In its heyday their mansion was by far the finest building in town. It is well worth exploring the recesses of the Posada Hidalgo hotel since, in many respects, it is a living museum with its entrance mural, antique furniture, sepia photographs and aging mementoes of earlier decades.

Allegedly, vast quantities of gold and silver lay buried under its floors and in the garden, but you can probably rest assured that any such treasures were dug up and invested elsewhere when Almada's mansion was remodeled into the present hotel. According to some, the spirit of Rafael Almada lives on. If you stay overnight, be prepared for strange noises and for the possibility that the ancient pianola suddenly bursts into a tune all by itself.

El Fuerte is a pleasant town to stroll around. Narrow streets, many lined by fine stone buildings, converge on the plaza. The church (with the tomb of Esteban Nicolás de la Vega y Colón de Portugal, the man who singlehandedly paid for its entire construction) is reputedly 18th century but many townhouses look considerably older. For example, Casa de los Alvarez (on Constitución, near its intersection with Juárez) has walls over a meter thick! Casa de los Constituyentes, on Calle Morelos, is also very old; this was the first House of Congress for the Western State.

On one side of the plaza is the Casa de la Cultura, occupying a building that was once a jail. The interior courtyard of the municipal palace (1903–1907) is out of all proportion, fit for a much larger town, and built when Rafael Almada was Mayor and Political Prefect of the district. Most commercial activity is not on the plaza but down the side streets. As for cuisine, El Fuerte is famous for fresh largemouth bass (from nearby reservoirs) and for barley water (*agua de cebada*), a flavorful mixture of barley, sugar, cinnamon and vanilla.

Even in the last century, El Fuerte played an important part in national history. In November 1915, in the midst of the Mexican Revolution, Carranza fought and defeated the legendary Pancho Villa here, a defeat that marked the beginning of the end for Villa's famed División del Norte.

From El Fuerte, side trips can be arranged to visit the Máscara mountains with their petroglyphs (a short hike on the other side of the Fuerte river), Isla de los Pajaros ("Bird Island"), and to Mayo Indian missions like Bayema and Tehueco ("Blue Sky"), founded in 1648. Another Indian village, Capomos, is noteworthy for its rustic earthenware pots and pans. An unpaved secondary road, formerly a stagecoach route, links El Fuerte to the attractive former mining town of Alamos (90 kilometers away) where lovingly-restored stone mansions have been transformed into boutique hotels and stores.

12

The Manila Connection: cultural exchange

In 1559 King Philip II of Spain ordered a fleet to be prepared to sail west from New Spain (Mexico) to the Philippines. Barra de Navidad, on the shores of Jalisco, was one of the centers of New Spain's maritime activity at the time. It offered a sandy beach in a well-protected bay, with tall forests inland from which to source the necessary timber. As the Spanish fleet was readied, Barra de Navidad echoed to the sounds of hammering and sawing.

All western Mexico was mobilized to support the venture. Roads were built to ferry supplies to the Barra de Navidad shipyards from the city of Guadalajara. To this day, the main Guadalajara-Barra de Navidad road is known as The Philippines Way. Food, planks, sails and rigging—all had to be acquired and transported to the port.

Every village had to support the effort, which was not without its dangers. For example, the Indians from Ameca complained of "many killed in the transport of rigging to Puerto de la Navidad where they are building ships."

The friendship spanning more than 450 years between Mexico and the Philippines began at 3:00am on 21 November 1564 when the expedition finally set sail. The expedition's commander, López de Legazpi, did not reveal their true destination to his sailors until the ships were well under way. He feared a mutiny since no previ-

ous expedition had ever managed to find its way back across the Pacific Ocean.

The expedition landed in the Philippines in March 1565. When López de Legazpi decided to remain there, he put his 17-year-old grandson in charge of guiding the ships back to Mexico. In one of the most amazing feats of sailing of all time, his grandson was successful, but when the expedition reached Acapulco in October the crew was too exhausted to drop anchor. The return voyage had cost more than 350,000 gold pesos in total and is commemorated today by a simple monument in Barra de Navidad's small plaza.

The Spanish authorities soon decided that bringing Asian goods back to Spain from their colony in the Philippines via Mexico, even though it entailed crossing the Pacific, transshipping the cargo across Mexico and then sailing from Veracruz to Spain, was safer than any alternative. Barra de Navidad soon became a regular port of call for Spanish sailors plying the so-called China route between Acapulco and Manila. To enable easier communication between Mexico City and Acapulco, a Camino Real (Royal Road) was built between Mexico City and Acapulco, initially used by pack mules. A road suitable for wheeled vehicles between these cities was not completed until well into the 20th century.

For 250 years, Spanish galleons carried Mexican silver to Manila and returned with spices, silk, porcelain, lacquerware and other exotic goods from the Orient. These "China galleons" displaced 2000 tons and were the largest seafaring vessels of their time in the world.

But the lure of easy treasure drew pirates such as Englishman Francis Drake. In 1579 Drake sacked the small port of Huatulco, now a premier multimillion-dollar tourist resort in the state of Oaxaca, and attacked the Manila galleon off the coast of California, exposing the vulnerability of Spanish sea traffic. For the next forty years, all the west coast ports, including Barra de Navidad, saw more pirates and corsairs than was good for them. Then, slowly but surely, the center of colonial operations moved further north into Sinaloa and Baja California.

The China galleons greatly stimulated spatial interactions between Acapulco and Manila, 15,000 kilometers away. Many Mexicans settled in Manila and scores of Nahuatl words entered Tagalog, the main Filipino language. These included *atole*, *avocado*, *balsa*, cacao, calabaza, *camote*, *chico*, chocolate, coyote, *nanay*, *tatay*, *tocayo* and *zapote*.

As well as vocabulary, some aspects of Mexican cuisine, customs and dress were also introduced to the Philippines, along with a variety of plants and flowers. In addition, the Filipino currency has the same name as Mexico's: the peso.

A large number of Filipino sailors migrated in the other direction, escaping from a life of servitude aboard a galleon by jumping ashore on the coasts of Colima and Guerrero. One sizable Filipino community settled in Coyuca, on Mexico's Costa Grande, 50 kilometers north of Acapulco. At one point in its early history Coyuca was known as Filipino Town.

The Filipinos who settled in Mexico introduced a game called *cara y cruz* (heads and tails) and a new fruit, the mango. Mangoes have become a bone of contention between the two countries. The first mango seedlings came to Mexico more than two hundred years ago. Since then selective breeding and plant crossing have turned Manila mangoes, as they are known, into much-desired, pale-yellow mangoes with a delicate skin and intensely juicy flesh. Mexican growers have requested that these mangoes be given denomination of origin status, despite their Filipino origin. The Philippines has lodged an official objection. The outcome of this dispute will not change Mexico's position as the world's leading exporter of mangoes, since the Manila variety is harder to handle and accounts for less than one percent of all Mexico's mango exports.

Filipino settlers in Mexico were known locally as Chinese Indians and also brought their expertise in the cultivation and use of palm trees. In Tagalog, palm fronds are known as *palapa*. By the end of the 18th century this name was in use, too, for the palm-roofed shelters which remain a distinctive style of architecture along Mexico's coasts.

The coconut palm's sap is still known locally as *tuba*, another Tagalog word. Filipino newcomers fermented the coconut wine made from this sap to produce a potent drink. Henry Bruman, a University of California geographer, documented how Filipino seamen on the Manila Galleon also introduced simple stills for making coconut brandy into western Mexico during the late 16th century. These techniques were quickly adopted by people in Mexico in order to distill the juice of their native agave plants into tequila. This is an excellent example of how developments in transportation can encourage cultural exchanges, and diminish the social, economic and cultural distance between places.

The China Poblana, the traditional style of dress worn by women in Mexico, still fashionable today, is supposedly named after a "Chinese" woman who arrived from the East as a slave during the early 1600s and subsequently captured the hearts and minds of the people of Puebla. However, according to some historians, it is far more likely she was actually a Filipino noblewoman who had arrived in Mexico aboard one of the Spanish galleons.

Mexico's independence from Spain (1821) brought an end to regular trans-Pacific contacts via the Manila–Acapulco galleons. Mexico's trade across the Pacific Ocean diminished, even as independence stimulated the development of new shipping routes from the Gulf coast port of Veracruz to such destinations as New Orleans and New York.

The friendship between Mexico and the Philippines has remained close down the years. For instance, in the second world war, several Mexican air force pilots in the elite Escuadrón 201 were sent by the U.S. government to assist their colleagues in the Philippines. The Filipino government later decorated the pilots for their heroism.

One curious and more recent link between the two countries is a plant known as divine sage. According to the Philippine Drug Enforcement Agency (PDEA), this is the Philippines' least desired import from Mexico, because of its significant public health risk. The plant is endemic to the remote region of the Sierra Mazateca in Oaxaca, Mexico, but now grows wild near Quezon City in the Philippines. The PDEA says that dried leaves of divine sage (*Salvia divinorum*), a member of the mint family, are hallucinogenic when chewed, sniffed or smoked. The plant's active ingredient, salvinorin A., is alleged to be the world's most potent naturally-occurring psychoactive compound by mass.

That probably explains why, in its native Oaxaca where divine sage grows in the warm, damp tropical evergreen and cloud forests at elevations between 300 and 1800 meters (1000 to 6000 feet), the local Mazatec people have a long tradition of employing it in spiritual healing ceremonies.

Despite its known hallucinogenic qualities, the cultivation and possession of divine sage remain legal in almost every country in the world. Even in the U.S., only certain states have criminalized the plant. Divine sage is just one more link in the long history of close connections between Mexico and the Philippines.

13

Birth of the Mexican Navy

An early story by science fiction and travel author Jules Verne was set in Mexico. Incredible as it may seem, he wrote it without ever having set foot in the country.

Jules Verne (1828–1905) is best known as one of the pioneers of science fiction writing. His most famous works include *Twenty Thousand Leagues Under the Sea*, a submarine voyage with Captain Nemo as the enigmatic hero; *A Journey to the Center of the Earth*, in which Professor Lidenbrock and his nephew Axel descend into an extinct volcano in Iceland and discover an underground world; and *From the Earth to the Moon*, a vivid forerunner of future space travel.

Verne's other popular works include *Around the World in Eighty Days*, in which eccentric Englishman Phileas Fogg races round the world in an effort to win a wager; *Five Weeks in a Balloon*, in which the heroes drift across unexplored areas in Central Asia; and *The Mysterious Island*.

Less well known is the fact that one of Verne's very first published stories was set in Mexico. Originally called "Les Premiers Navires de la Marine Mexicaine" (The First Ships of the Mexican Navy), it was published in 1851, when Verne was only 23 years old. It is one of the few stories for which Verne never received any payment.

Having never visited Mexico, Verne relied for his background information on the tales he heard from seafarers in his native port of Nantes, and on the recollections of Jacques Arago, a friend in Paris who had fought in Mexico's War of Independence. Verne had a lifelong interest in the sea; both his parents were seafarers. As a young boy, he had run off, hoping to become a cabin boy, but was found and returned to his parents.

In 1847 Verne went to Paris to study law. The following year the February Revolution broke out and, after his uncle introduced him into literary and creative circles, the young man decided to forgo his career in law to focus on writing.

"The First Ships of the Mexican Navy" is set in 1825. Shortly after independence from Spain in 1821, Mexico recognized the need for a strong navy to protect its extensive territory, which then included California and stretched as far south as present-day Costa Rica. Mexico's first Secretary of War and Navy, appointed in 1821, was Antonio de Medina, who had fought at the Battle of Trafalgar in 1805. He urged the Mexican Congress to prioritize the formation of a navy. Though de Medina could not have known it at the time, a series of foreign interventions later in the 19th century would confirm the vital importance of Mexico building up and maintaining a strong naval presence.

Verne's story is based on real life events, even if the timing of them is changed. It explains how the Mexican Navy obtained its first two warships. As Verne tells it, "On October 18, 1825, Spanish ship of the line *Asia* and eight-gun brig *Constanzia* lay off Aguijan, one of the Marianas." The crews of these vessels, badly fed, ill-paid, and overwhelmed with fatigue during their six months voyage for Spain, have been secretly plotting a mutiny.

Off the coast of Mexico, Lieutenant Martínez, seaman José and their associates take command of the two Spanish warships, intending to sell them to the republican government of Mexico, which lacks any navy and is desperate to protect its ports. When two of their conspirators disappear, Martínez and José race across the country at full speed, hoping to reach the capital, Mexico City, as quickly as possible, in order to preempt any attempt that their missing comrades may make to strike their own bargain. The exciting pursuit, during which the heroes survive even an avalanche, builds to an inevitable climax.

The wide range of locales used in the story include four of Mexico's Pacific coast ports—Acapulco, San Blas, Zacatula and Tehuantepec—as well as the towns of Cigualan [Cihuatlán], Chilpanzingo [Chilpancingo], Taxco, Cacahuimilchan and Cuernavaca. They also include Popocatepetl volcano and the pre–Hispanic site of Xochicalco.

In reality, the events unfolded in March 1825, rather than October. The *Asia* and the *Constante*, along with other ships, were sailing from Peru to the Philippines when they anchored off Omaja on the island of Guam. Poor conditions and lack of pay led to a mutiny which put First Lieutenant José Martínez in charge. On 28 April the ships put into the port of Monterey (Upper California) and the crews agreed to exchange the ships and swear loyalty to Mexico in exchange for a payment equivalent to the back pay they were owed, together with the right to live wherever they wanted. From Monterey, they sailed to Acapulco. At this point, the ships became officially part of the Mexican Navy. With new crews, the *Asia*, now renamed the *Congreso Mexicano*, set off with the *Constante* to sail round Cape Horn and challenge the Spanish ships still stationed at San Juan de Ulúa, off Veracruz.

By the time they finally arrived on 9 March 1827, they were too late; the Spanish ships had already left. The *Congreso Mexicano* was then used as a floating warehouse and later a prison ship before it sank in 1832. The *Constante* fared no better. It returned to the Pacific coast, but also sank in 1832, in the port of San Blas, where the wreck obstructed navigation into the port to such an extent that it was towed further out to sea two years later.

The complete title given by Verne to his story was "North America. Historical studies. The first ships of the Mexican Navy."

Meticulous as he was in regards to his geography, Verne was understandably very upset when the publisher changed North America to South America without first seeking his permission!

As Verne's writing career took off, he spent countless hours in Parisian libraries eagerly pursuing his interests in geography, geology, engineering and astronomy. His wide-ranging knowledge would subsequently be used to great effect in his many full length novels. From the mid 1860s onwards, Verne was increasingly successful and wealthy. He reworked "The First Ships of the Mexican Navy" in 1876 to include it in his *Extraordinary Voyages* series as "A Drama in Mexico."

To this day, Jules Verne remains the most widely read French author of all time, and one of the most translated authors in the world. Despite its now out-of-date science, his *Extraordinary Voyages* series still captures the imagination of many young readers.

The Mexican Navy (*Secretaría de Marina*) has also grown, and now has about 56,000 personnel, operating 200 ships and 100 aircraft. Its main tasks are to protect oil reserves in the Gulf of Mexico, assist in the fight against drug traffickers, and to aid in disaster relief efforts.

14

U.S. appropriates Cinco de Mayo

Of the many battles fought on Mexican soil in the 19th century, only one—the Battle of Puebla, fought on 5 May 1862—has given rise to a national day of celebration in Mexico, a day when schools and banks are closed.

Why this one? The main reason is that the Battle of Puebla marks Mexico's only major military success since independence from Spain in 1821. Mexico has never been considered a military power. In the 19th century, France, Spain, Britain and the U.S. all hatched or carried out plans to invade. Mexico's 19th-century history is a catalog of repeated interventions by foreign powers in its internal affairs.

The first French invasion, the so-called Pastry War in 1838, lasted only a few days. A decade later, U.S. troops entered Mexico City, and Mexico was forced to cede Texas, New Mexico and (Upper) California—in all, some 2 million square kilometers (half its territory)—in exchange for $15 million pesos.

In 1857 Mexico proclaimed a new constitution. This led to the Reform War (1858–60) between the liberals, led by Benito Juárez, who supported the new constitution, and the conservatives, who opposed it. The war decimated the country's labor force, reduced economic development and cost a small fortune, leaving both sides with serious financial problems.

In 1859 Juárez (in Veracruz) published Reform laws which nationalized church property and established the separation of church and state. Later laws established civil marriages, a civil registry, and proclaimed the right to freedom of worship. The Reform War ended in 1860. Pro-liberal forces, led by General González Ortega, finally occupied Mexico City on 1 Jan 1861. The conservatives went into hiding, but would reappear shortly afterwards, supporting another French invasion.

President Juárez took office to find that the public coffers were empty. He expelled several diplomats and some clerics and tried to nationalize church estates. Resistance was stiff. Juárez believed that Reform would eventually solve the country's financial problems, but his administration was short of cash. On 17 July 1861, in a desperate attempt to avoid bankruptcy, Mexico suspended all payments on its foreign debt for two years, infuriating foreign powers.

Three months later, Britain, France and Spain decided to seize the port of Veracruz on Mexico's Gulf coast and obtain payment by force. In December, 6000 Spanish soldiers landed, followed a month later by 7000 British marines and 2000 French troops.

At this point, France demanded that Mexico repay $12 million pesos, an absurdly large sum, and one well beyond Mexico's means. Juárez negotiated and, satisfied that their demands would soon be met, England and Spain withdrew their forces. France, however, had bigger plans, and decided to stay.

To understand why the French remained, a little backstory is needed. France's emperor, Napoleon III (Louis Napoleon Bonaparte) had grand ambitions. Urged on by his Spanish wife, Eugénie, Napoleon envisaged French influence spreading throughout the Americas. He wanted to impose a monarchy, construct a canal and railroad across the Isthmus of Tehuantepec, and limit U.S. expansionism. To achieve these lofty ambitions, Napoleon needed a suitable puppet for the Mexican throne, and he had the perfect candidate: Austrian archduke Maximilian von Habsburg.

In Mexico, the French troops had moved inland from Vera-cruz. While final details were being negotiated, the French agreed to withdraw back to the coast. Instead of doing this, however, they occupied the city of Orizaba, and then routed a Mexican force which tried to hold the pass of Aculzingo.

Mexico had nowhere to turn. It was unable to call on U.S. assistance as that country was in the throws of its own Civil War. Its president, Abraham Lincoln, was sympathetic but not in a position to help.

The French Army was supremely confident that they could crush any enemy militarily. Since tasting defeat at Waterloo in 1815, the French had won battles in Europe and Asia, and were unbeaten in almost fifty years. Paul Vanderwood quotes the French Commander, Charles Ferdinand Latrille, the Count of Lorencez, as boasting that: "We are so superior to the Mexicans in race, organization, morality and devoted sentiments that I beg your excellency [the Minster of War] to inform the Emperor that as the head of 6000 soldiers I am already master of Mexico."

Marching from Orizaba toward Mexico City, the French needed to secure Puebla, defended by 4000 or so ill-equipped Mexican soldiers. Ironically, given the subsequent outcome, many of the defenders were armed with antiquated weapons that had seen service at Waterloo prior to being purchased in 1825 by Mexico's ambassador to London at a bargain basement price. The Mexican forces, the Army of the East (*Ejército de Oriente*), were commanded by General Ignacio Zaragoza, a Texas-born Mexican.

Fifteen years earlier, 30,000 Mexican troops, commanded by General Antonio López de Santa Anna, had failed to contain 6000 U.S. soldiers under General Winfield Scott. How could just 4000 Mexican soldiers hope to contain the mighty French Army? General Zaragoza realized that the odds looked poor, but dug his forces into defensive positions centered on the twin forts of Loreto and Guadalupe. The Loreto fort is now the Museum of No Intervention (*Museo de la No Intervención*), complete with toy soldiers, set in an area of parkland that also houses a museum of regional history and a planetarium.

On Cinco de Mayo (5 May) 1862, Zaragoza issued orders that his commanders—Generals Felipe B. Berriozabal, Porfirio Díaz, Félix Díaz, Miguel Negrete and Francisco de Lamadrid—must repel the invaders at all costs.

The French launched a brief artillery bombardment, but soon found that the uneven field where the fighting was taking place had become so muddy from heavy unseasonable downpours that maneuvering their heavy weapons was next to impossible. Bullets rained down on them from the Mexican troops occupying the higher ground near the forts. At noon, the French commander, General Lorencez, ordered his troops to charge through the center of the Mexican lines, but his plan failed. The lines held strong, and the non-stop musket fire began to take its toll. The French tried again: two more determined attacks were similarly rebuffed.

That afternoon, the Mexican forces counterattacked, spurred on by well-organized cavalry led by Porfirio Díaz, who would subsequently serve almost thirty years as President of Mexico. The afternoon wore on. When the smoke cleared, it was apparent that the defenders of Puebla had successfully repelled the European invaders.

The French troops fled back to Orizaba, where Zaragoza attacked again. This time, the French scuttled down to the coast to regroup. A crack European army had been soundly defeated by a motley collection of machete-wielding peasants from the war-torn republic of Mexico. In consequence, a few days later, President Juárez declared that Cinco de Mayo would henceforth be a national day of celebration.

Meanwhile, back in Paris, Napoleon was enraged. He ordered massive reinforcements and sent a 27,000 strong force of French military might to help place Maximilian on the throne of Mexico.

The strengthened French army (under Marshal Elie Forey) took Mexico City in 1863, forcing Juárez and his supporters to flee. Juárez established himself in Paso del Norte (now El Paso) on the U.S. border, from where he continued to orchestrate resistance to the French presence.

Supported by the conservatives, Maximilian was placed on the throne in May 1864. By this time, in the U.S., the Unionists had taken Vicksburg and the U.S. government was considering its position. In May 1865 General Philip Sheridan moved 50,000 soldiers to the border to ensure that French troops did not advance any further north. Diplomatic pressure for a French withdrawal intensified and Napoleon III finally agreed to remove his troops in February 1866. The last French forces set sail back to Europe in March 1867.

Soon after their departure, Juárez reestablished Republican government in Mexico, and put Maximilian on trial, ending an extraordinary period in Mexican history.

In Mexico, Cinco de Mayo is celebrated with lengthy parades in the state and city of Puebla, and in neighboring states such as Veracruz, but there are no great celebrations in most of the rest of the country. Almost every Mexican town and city, however, has at least one street called Cinco de Mayo.

North of the border, in the U.S., Cinco de Mayo has been transformed into a much more popular cultural event. Many communities use Cinco de Mayo as the perfect excuse to celebrate everything Mexican: food, music, drinks, dancing, crafts and customs. Cinco de Mayo has become a very significant commercial event, one now celebrated with much more intensity north of the border than in Mexico itself.

15

Railroads helped forge the nation

Among the road signs in Mexico that are quite cryptic to foreign visitors are those that begin "Est." followed by a name. In this context, "Est." stands for *Estación* (Railroad Station). Even though very few passenger trains now run in Mexico, the sign is still commonly seen when traveling in many parts of the country.

If you follow the sign, you are likely to be rewarded by finding an historic building, since most of the country's railroad lines were built at the end of the 19th century. Many Mexican railroad stations date from that time and some are wonderful architectural monuments to a (sadly) bygone age.

Turning down an "Est." side road can be the beginning of a real adventure, with plenty of historical footnotes waiting to be revealed. The station buildings are often period pieces. The largest cities had two-story stations. Some are distinctly *norteamericano* in style, looking as if they were transplanted in their entirety from the Midwest or Prairies. Others are much more European, perhaps French or British. The differences, of course, are due to the sources of capital employed and the nationalities of the principal shareholders of the many different companies responsible for their construction.

When in the general vicinity of a station, look out for old railroad cars and engines. In some places boxcars have been transformed into desirable residences with flower-bedecked porches. Former engines, polished and gleaming, may have become permanent traffic islands controlling the flow of motor vehicles outside the station entrance. Other locomotives and wagons have been left to rust in abandoned sidings.

The names of some stations are far from ordinary. For example, in San Luis Potosí, there is the authentically-1930s Estación Wadley, an interesting name given that W (pronounced doble-oo) doesn't even exist as a letter in the Spanish alphabet, leading to the virtual absence of entries under W in the Spanish side of any bilingual dictionary. Most W words in Spanish—such as *weekend*, *whisky*, and *wafle*—are recent imports. Wadley is named for William Wadley, a U.S. railroad entrepreneur involved in this line's construction.

Further south, in the state of Puebla, is the equally improbably named Est. Honey, named for English engineer Richard Honey, who came to Mexico from Cornwall in 1862 and made his immense wealth through mining and railroad interests. Honey built Mexico's first iron bridge, spanning the River Tula at Taxquillo, and was a cofounder of Mexico City's Jockey Club and Reforma Athletic Club. He was also a close friend and confidante of President Porfirio Díaz, who gave Honey the nickname *Gran Bretaña* (Great Britain).

Díaz aggressively encouraged rail development through generous concessions and government subsidies to foreign investors. By 1884 Mexico had 12,000 kilometers of track, including a U.S.-financed link from Ciudad Juárez in Chihuahua to Torreón and Mexico City. A British company built lines from Mexico City to Guadalajara, and from Mexico City to Nuevo Laredo via Monterrey. Links to San Luis Potosí, Monterrey, Tampico and other points soon followed. The Mexican Revolution (1910–1920) halted railroad building, and the government priority shifted to roads, but a west coast railroad from Sonora to Guadalajara was finally completed in 1927. Decades later, the Yucatán Peninsula was joined to the national network and, in 1961, the famous Chihuahua to Los Mochis line through the Copper Canyon was finally completed.

Railroads revolutionized Mexico. The railroad was five to ten times faster than any earlier form of transport. Railroads lowered freight costs by roughly 80 percent and shrank the size of Mexico in terms of travel time; they were both cheaper and more comfortable than stagecoaches.

The railroad era ushered in an entire new genre of travel writing, which culminated in the first genuine guidebooks describing routes and places that travelers could visit with relative ease. The earliest comprehensive guide to Mexico, *Appletons' Guide to Mexico* (1883), was quickly followed by others.

At the start of the 20th century, cities with favorable rail connections grew significantly while those without tended to stagnate. Railroads brought speed and economies of scale that encouraged mass production for the national market. For example, cotton growing on irrigated farms near Torreón expanded rapidly because the harvest could be shipped easily and cheaply by rail to the large textile factories in Guadalajara, Puebla and Orizaba. Finished textiles were then distributed, also by rail, throughout the country.

In the second half of the 20th century the rapidly improving road network meant railroads faced growing competition for passenger travel from cars and buses. The advent of air travel gave passengers even more options, and railroad traffic went into decline. The current system, with roughly 21,000 kilometers of track, mainly for freight, is far less important to Mexico's economy than it was a century ago.

Since the privatization of the railroad system in 1995, many secondary rail lines have been abandoned. Much of Mexico's historic railroad infrastructure lies in ruins, but some former lines have been turned into walking and cycling trails. The state of Jalisco, for instance, is reconditioning 120 kilometers (75 miles) of former rail routes as Green Route trails for hikers and cyclists.

Some old stations along these routes, including Ameca, a lovely building dating back more than a century, are being restored to provide exhibition space and basic services.

As part of an unusual geo-art project, two intrepid Mexican artists, Ivan Puig and Andres Padilla Domene, built a vehicle capable of traveling on either roads or train tracks and used it to explore some of the country's abandoned lines. The photographs they took along the way, and interviews they had with people they met, formed the basis for a 2014 exhibit at the Furtherfield Gallery in London, England.

Mexico has about a thousand railroad stations with permanent buildings, half of them listed as having architectural, cultural or artistic value. Several former stations are now rail museums, including León and Acámbaro (both in Guanajuato), Aguascalientes, Torreón (Coahuila), Oaxaca, Puebla, Mérida (Yucatán), Tulancingo (Hidalgo) and Xalapa (Veracruz). The magnificent, two-story former railroad station in Chapala is now a cultural center.

The oldest purpose-built railroad station in Mexico dates back to 1869 and is in the city of Puebla. However, in the nearby spa town of Cuautla, Morelos, a much older building, a 17th-century friary, was adapted for use as a station. By most accounts, this is the oldest building still in use as a railroad station anywhere in the world. A short section of narrow gauge line between Cuautla and Yecapiztla reopened in 1986 for a tourist steam train service, with Baldwin locomotive #279, first brought into service in 1904, pulling four restored second class coaches.

Railroad stations in Mexico are throwbacks to an earlier age and any of those that merit an "Est." signpost from the highway are probably worth visiting. One of the most memorable experiences I've ever had after taking an "Est." detour was in the 1980s, in the southern state of Oaxaca, where I found that the public shuttle-bus from a small village to the local railroad station was an ox-drawn cart. Passengers, including several women in the beautiful, traditional, hand-embroidered, full-length dresses typical of the Tehuantepec region, stood regally in the open cart, despite being enveloped in a cloud of dust as the animals plodded along the dirt track.

Some years earlier, in the same general region, one entire wall of the handsome brick-built station at Matías Romero still proudly displayed the same menu (and prices) that passengers had enjoyed in its restaurant in the 1930s.

Following an "Est." sign can be an easy, unlisted and fun side trip to bring you unexpected glimpses into Mexico's fascinating past.

16

Utopian experiment in Sinaloa

The port of Topolobampo and nearby city of Los Mochis ("Mo-chees" in local parlance) in the northern state of Sinaloa, are two of Mexico's newer cities. Their story dates back only as far as 1872, when U.S. engineer Albert Kimsey Owen arrived. Owen envisaged Topolobampo as the center for a utopian U.S. colony based on sugarcane production in this previously unsettled area and as the terminus for a railroad across the Western Sierra Madre.

Owen had been raised in New Harmony, the city founded by Robert Owen (no relation), and decided to try and found a similar "ideal socialist" city somewhere in Mexico. In 1868, at the age of 21, he visited Veracruz, but failed to find a suitable loca-tion. In 1870 he was commissioned by General William Palmer, who owned the Denver–Rio Grande Railroad and was planning a railroad line south into Mexico, to explore the route for a rail-road running north to the U.S. along the west coast of Mexico. Owen explored the Pacific coast, learning Spanish as he went. In Mazatlán in 1871 the local American consul, Benjamin Carman, told him about a splendid natural harbor further north called, by the natives, Ohuira ("Enchanted place").

By 1872 Owen had decided that Carman was correct and that the shores of Ohuira (now known as Topolobampo, "the lion's watering place" or "tiger's water") were ideal for his purpose. He imagined a modern port city there, with boats setting off across the ocean to Asia. Owen decided that the original plan for a railroad along Mexico's Pacific coast was far inferior to the idea of an international railroad link from Kansas, via Missouri and Texas, to this wonderful port of Topolobampo. Even though the railroad had to cross the rugged Western Sierra Madre, its construction would cut days (and dollars) off all trade between the U.S. and countries bordering the Pacific Ocean. The Panama Canal had not yet been built and a Kansas–Topolobampo railroad would save at least 960 kilometers (600 miles) compared to alternative routes.

Owen promptly founded the Texas, Topolobampo and Pacific Railroad and Telegraph Company (later the American and Mexican Pacific Railroad) and returned to the U.S. to seek financing to turn his vision into reality. After seven fruitless years, he met Porfirio Díaz (Mexico's president for almost thirty years) and, in 1881, was granted the concession to establish a Utopian city, initially called Ciudad González, but whose name was later changed to Pacific City and then Topolobampo. Today, Topolobampo is one of the most important fishing and freight ports on Mexico's Pacific coast.

To finance his plans, Owen launched a company called The Credit Foncier of Sinaloa, and issued 200,000 bonds, sold for $10 each. Half the proceeds were intended to pay for the railroad, half for the new city. Owen also started a similarly-named newspaper, published in Hammonton, New Jersey, in order to disseminate his ideas, which included the suppression of both private property and private means of production. Owen argued that, instead of money, residents would gain credit for work. Houses were to be built collectively, as were roads, schools, hospitals, libraries, universities, factories, irrigation schemes, and everything else required to make the settlement as self-supporting as possible.

Many families signed up to move to Mexico and help Owen realize his dream. After settlement began in October 1886, the flow of Americans southwards was far greater than Owen had envisaged, or had prepared for, so the early settlers were forced to improvise to meet their housing and water needs.

Two and a half years later, in April 1889, the first large group of colonists—300-strong—set sail from New York, arriving in Sinaloa in July, only to find a deserted beach and no Owen. Owen had returned to the U.S. to raise funds but finally came back to Topolobampo the following year with another 30 colonists. During 1891, 70 more settlers arrived.

Owen's group founded various settlements, including Vega-town (Estación Vega), La Logia, El Público and El Platt. The new settlers dug, largely by hand, a massive, 12-kilometer-long irrigation canal called Los Tastes, to divert water from the Fuerte River to flow across their lands, and busied themselves preparing everything for large-scale cultivation. But problems abounded and, despite their heroic efforts, the project was derailed. The canal did not work as intended, and pumping was needed to move the water. Rather than the start of something great, the canal turned out to be the beginning of the end as the germ of capitalism took over. After the canal was filled in 1892, some colonists, known as "Kikers", asked for land ownership, but Owen and his followers, the "Saints", refused. Despite a meeting convened in New York to try to thrash out differences over water rights, quotas and prices, some settlers sold their shares and left.

In all, in 1892, more than 200 settlers gave up, disillusioned as a result of the hard work, hunger and disease. The following year, a sawmill was installed, to build U.S.-style homes. The colonists tried to bring more than a thousand large tree trunks across the mountains, floating them along the Fuerte River, but lost almost all of them when the river's strong current drove them past the port and into the Gulf of California.

The final straw came when Owen, instead of paying the Mexican government for the concession as he had agreed, used the group's limited funds to start building the railroad across the sierra to Texas. Shortly afterwards, officials cancelled the concession and handed it instead to an out-and-out capitalist, Benjamin Francis Johnston, who quickly put an end to the socialist experiment.

In November 1893 Owen finally gave up. He and almost all of the 1200 *norteamericanos* who had visited or tried to eke out a living here made their way back home. Despite Owen's failure to complete either the port or the railroad, the experimental settlement at Topolobampo had, nevertheless, laid the groundwork for the subsequent agricultural transformation of the Fuerte Valley floodplain into one of the most productive farming regions in all of Mexico.

Even before the Utopian settlers returned to the U.S. in 1893, Johnston, from Virginia, had founded the Compañia Azucarera Aguila S.A. [Eagle Sugar Co.] and built a sugar factory, church, airport, dam and the Memory Hill lighthouse. Ten years later, in 1903, he officially founded Los Mochis, a name which means place of the land turtles.

Johnston eventually came to own more than 200,000 hectares, and built a veritable palace (including a banquet kitchen, indoor pool and even an elevator, one of the first in the country) for his residence in the town. The mansion had lavish furnishings and was surrounded by a huge garden, full of exotic plants—which later became the city's botanical gardens, Parque Sinaloa. During the Mexican Revolution (1910–1920), Johnston, who was owner or part-owner of no fewer than 22 companies at the time, even printed his own money. Sadly, after Johnston died in 1937 in Hong Kong, his family left Mexico for the U.S. His luxurious house was later torn down and the area redeveloped for a modern shopping plaza.

Los Mochis became especially important as a major commercial center in the second half of the 20th century, marketing much of the produce grown on the bountiful, irrigated floodplain of the Fuerte River. A large proportion of this produce is exported to the U.S. via the famous Copper Canyon railroad. Los Mochis is the passenger terminus at the western end of the railroad line.

For freight, the line continues to the city's port, Topolobampo, with its shrimp-packing plant and all the normal dockside installations. The port's location, on a superb natural harbor, the head of a drowned river valley, or ria, affords excellent protection for ships in the event of hurricanes.

The motives of both Owen, who died in 1916, and Johnston have been questioned by many historians who view Owen's efforts as being more akin to capitalism and neo-imperialism than any form of socialism. Owen's projects, they argue, might have resulted in the annexation of 1,000,000 square kilometers (386,000 square miles) to a U.S. which had ambitious expansionist ideas at the time. Owen has been labeled variously a visionary, madman, con man or swindler. Johnston, meanwhile, has also been regarded by some as a stooge for those in the U.S. who favored expansionism.

Both Topolobampo and Los Mochis are unusual compared with most other towns in Mexico in that they were established relatively recently in locations where there were no pre-existing settlements. As luck would have it, idealistic failure in Topolobampo led to capitalist success in Los Mochis.

17

Historic aerial bombing of warship

Captain Gustavo Salinas Camiña was the first man in the world to bomb a warship from an airplane. This momentous event occurred in 1914 in the vicinity of Topolobampo in Sinaloa.

The bombing took place at a time when the nature of warfare was changing dramatically. Warring factions, previously forced to rely on only land and sea forces, saw the deployment of aircraft as a powerful new weapon, one capable of rewriting the best tactics to use against their adversaries.

The earliest adoption of air power for fighting was when an Italian pilot Giulo Gavoti threw grenades out of his Blériot XI in the general direction of a Turkish camp in Libya in November 1911. The following year, a Belgian pilot dropped bombs on a Turkish military base during the Balkan Wars. In August 1914 General Erich Ludendorff is credited with ordering the first air raid in history, when he called in zeppelins to bomb the city and forts of Liège in Belgium.

The history of aerial warfare was also being written in Mexico, where the success of the Wright brothers and other pioneers in the U.S. had attracted considerable attention. In 1908 Alfredo Robles Domínguez had published his *Tratado de locomoción aérea* (*Treatise of Aerial Locomotion*). In 1909 the Society for the Promotion of Aviation (Sociedad Impulsora de la Aviación) was established in

Mexico City. On 8 January 1910, a young Mexican, Alberto Braniff successfully made Mexico's first flight at the Balbuena airfield in Mexico City. His 60-horsepower Voisin biplane flew 500 meters and reached a maximum height of 25 meters.

Alberto Braniff was the son of wealthy U.S.-born industrialist and railroad entrepreneur Thomas Braniff. Alberto was sent to study in France, where he learned to fly and acquired the French-built airplane which he brought back to Mexico. The family of this pioneer aviator owned a mansion in Mexico City and a holiday home (now the well-known Cazadores restaurant) at Lake Chapala. The Braniffs were members of Mexico's elite, embedded in high society and close friends with President Díaz and his entourage. Incidentally, and despite the coincidence of name and common interest in flying, Alberto Braniff and his brother Tomás were not related in any way to the Thomas Elmer Braniff who (with his brother Paul) founded Braniff Airlines in Oklahoma in the late 1920s.

After the Mexican Revolution broke out, Díaz resigned. In 1911 Francisco I. Madero took over the presidency. Madero was a visionary supporter of aviation, and the first head of state anywhere in the world to brave a flight in an aircraft. Madero's interest had been piqued when he attended an international air show in March 1911 given by the Moisant International Aviators. Inspired by their impressive display of flying, President Madero took his own short historic flight in a Deperdussin airplane on 30 November 1911.

The Moisant International Aviators, often known as John Moisant's Flying Circus, play a key role in our story. John Moisant, taught to fly by Louis Blériot, designed, built and flew the first metal (aluminum) aircraft in 1909. With his brother Alfred, he then founded the Moisant International Aviators, a flying circus which went on a barnstorming tour of the U.S. and three cities in Mexico: Monterrey, Mexico City and Veracruz. Author Henry Villard described the flying circus as having "a dozen airplanes and their mechanics, and eight death-defying aviators". It traveled from city to city by special train with a built-in repair shop.

The circus was disbanded in 1911 after John Moisant was killed in a flying accident, and Alfred Moisant returned to New York, where he opened an aviation school at Hempstead Plains, near Garden City on Long Island.

This was precisely the time when President Madero was taking office in Mexico. Madero inherited a nation in turmoil, the early stages of the Mexican Revolution. Appreciating the potential role of aircraft in intelligence gathering, the president decided to acquire some planes of his own. Planes are no use without pilots, so Madero sponsored five young Mexicans to travel to Long Island, New York, to train at the Moisant International Aviators School. The "Famous Five", as they became known, were Gustavo Salinas Camiña, Alberto Salinas Carranza, Horacio Ruiz Gaviño, Juan Pablo Suárez and Eduardo Aldasoro Suárez.

Gustavo Salinas Camiña (1893–1964) received his first commercial license (number 172) from the Aero Club of America at Flushing Meadows, New York, in 1912, and was about to write his own page in aviation history.

All five young pilots completed their studies, gained their flying certificates, and returned to Mexico. Shortly afterwards, following a coup d'état, their patron, Madero, was assassinated and General Victoriano Huerta claimed power. Madero's followers retained support in northern Mexico, where they rallied behind Huerta's rival, General Venustiano Carranza, who assigned Salinas, and two of Mexico's newly acquired airplanes, to the command of General Álvaro Obregón.

In April 1914, one of Obregón's gunships, the *Tampico*, was sailing off the coast of Sinaloa, close to the port of Topolobampo, when it came under attack from two Huertista warships: the *Morelos* and the *Guerrero*. Obregón ordered Salinas to do something about it. On 14 April, accompanied by his mechanic Teodoro Madariaga, Salinas flew his Glenn Martin pusher-biplane *Sonora* over the *Guerrero* and began bombing it. The Huertista warships put out to sea, and the *Tampico* survived to fight another day. The *Tampico* was less lucky two months later, however, when it met the *Guerrero* again, caught fire and sank.

The action at the Battle of Topolobampo was the first naval-air skirmish in history. Aircraft had revolutionized the art of combat, and war would never be the same again.

The significance of this major shift in warfare was clearly not lost on Salinas himself. Many years later, in 1943, when he was chief of the Mexican Army Air Forces, he went on an inspection visit to Maxwell Field, Alabama. There, as quoted on Ralph Cooper's website *The Early Birds of Aviation*, Salinas recounted that, "The bombs I used were homemade, with a charge of 52 sticks of dynamite. Primitive as they were, they worked like a charm. At the time I was flying an old Wright pusher type. It occurred to me that the day would come when we would have planes of weight-carrying efficiency beyond one's fondest hopes, and that then the plane would come into its own as a military assault weapon of fabulous power. That day has come."

Gustavo Salinas Camiña, the first airman to bomb a warship, died on 5 March 1964, at the age of 70, and was buried in the public cemetery of Cuatro Ciénegas de Carranza in the state of Coahuila. He is among those remembered each year on 23 October, Mexico's National Aviation Day.

18

Deceptive national symbols

Every year, on the evening of 15 September, the ceremony of "El Grito" ("The shout") is held in towns and cities across the country, as Mexico celebrates her birthday, the anniversary of her independence from Spain.

For days prior to this celebration, sidewalks are taken over in a tide of nationalistic fervor by vendors selling national flags, toys and trinkets, as well as flowers and hollowed-out eggshells stuffed with flour. In Mexico City, so many people flock to the massive main square, or zócalo, in front of the National Palace that the crowd spills over into surrounding streets. The formal ceremony there is followed by a wild street party, best viewed (to avoid flour-bedecked hair and clothing) from one of the overlooking hotel balconies.

There are numerous curiosities associated with this celebration, some of which we explore here.

First, let's consider the date. The official holiday for Mexican independence is not 15 September, but 16 September. On that date, in 1810, Mexico's War of Independence began. In the early morning hours of that long-ago 16 September, Roman Catholic priest Miguel Hidalgo urged his parishioners in Dolores (now Dolores Hidalgo), in Guanajuato, to rise up and act. Eleven years of unrest preceded formal independence from Spain on 24 August

1821. Curiously, Mexico chose to celebrate independence on the anniversary of the day the Independence War started, rather than the day it was finally achieved. Every 16 September, the occasion is marked by street parades throughout the country.

At first sight, the decision to reenact El Grito on 15 September appears to be more a nod to citizens' convenience than historical veracity, but there is more to the story than that. Prior to 1910, many places held El Grito in the early hours of 16 September, but in that year President Porfirio Díaz decided that the centenary of Mexican independence should be celebrated in style. Díaz chose to perform the "traditional" Grito on 15 September because that day just happened to be both the Day of Saint Porfirio (an obscure fourth century Greek saint) and his own 80th birthday. Why not have one big bash and celebrate both President and country at the same time? Even though the Mexican Revolution broke out later that year (and Díaz eventually entered exile in Paris), Mexico continues to start its annual Independence Day celebrations on the evening of 15 September.

In Mexico City the President ends the El Grito ceremony each year by ringing the bell of the National Palace and praising the leaders of the independence movement before shouting "¡*Viva México!*" three times; onlookers roar and applaud in approval. Most people assume that this cry echoes what Father Miguel Hidalgo shouted to his parishioners in 1810, but this is ridiculed by historians, because Mexico as an entity did not exist prior to independence. Back in those days, New Spain, as it was then called, was one of the richest parts of the world, and actually very much larger in area than present-day Mexico, because it encompassed a massive area which became U.S. territory following the conclusion of the 1846–48 U.S. War with Mexico. While there is no academic consensus as to what Hidalgo actually said in 1810, there is common agreement that it could not, and did not, include the phrase "¡*Viva México!*"

On the night of El Grito, Mexican flags are everywhere, as they are on other national holidays. The flags, too, are beset with curiosities. The design has a central emblem of an eagle, serpent and cactus, set against three wide vertical stripes colored green, white and red. Every Mexican schoolchild learns, from kindergarten, what the colors signify: green is hope, white is unity and red is the blood of heroes. However, even this symbolism has changed over time. The original meaning of the colors in 1821 was green for independence, white for religion and red for union between Americans and Europeans. Since there is no law governing the interpretation of the colors, the current interpretation may change again in the future.

In other respects, the flag's design today is very similar to the design first adopted in 1821, with the exception that the eagle originally faced forwards, whereas it has faced sideways since 1916. The national symbols shown in the emblem of the flag are repeated on coins and elsewhere.

The central emblem on the flag and coins depicts an eagle, perched on a prickly-pear cactus and devouring a serpent. The cactus is growing on a rock that rises above a lake. The conventional version is that this unlikely combination represents the founding of the Aztec city of Tenochtitlan, now the national capital Mexico City. Tenochtitlan was originally founded in 1325 by the Mexica, an ancient tribe that originated somewhere in northern Mexico. According to legend, the Mexica were told by their gods to migrate southwards and build a new settlement where they saw the right signs. They would know they had found the right place when they found an eagle clutching a snake while perched on a nopal cactus. After years of wandering, they finally found this sign, on an island in the middle of a lake in central Mexico, and began building Tenochtitlan.

Certain details of this story may not be quite so straightforward as they seem. For starters, were the Mexica really looking for a place where an eagle, serpent and cactus coincided? All the known depictions of this legend date from after the Spanish conquest in the early 16th century. The earliest images of the founding of

Tenochtitlan, including that in the Codex Mendoza, show only an eagle perched on a cactus, with nothing in its talons. Even in those cases where the eagle does have something in its talons, the object is usually either a bird or a *tuna* (the fruit of the nopal). Attempts to put the various depictions in chronological order seem to indicate that those with a serpent are much more recent than those with a bird or tuna.

This has led some anthropologists to argue that the conventional story is a revisionist reinterpretation of history. The snake was added some time after the conquest, perhaps as a potent psychological reminder to the natives that their non-Christian religion, as represented by the serpent, had been crushed by Spanish military might, represented by the eagle.

To make the story even more confusing, the so-called "eagle" isn't really an eagle at all! The bird on the national coat-of-arms, like the bird depicted in ancient codices, is always shown as having a distinctive crest. The only eagles or members of the eagle family sporting a crest in Mexico are the harpy eagle and the various hawk-eagles; however, their range is confined to tropical southern Mexico. According to ornithologists, the most likely candidate for the bird shown on the national crest is the crested caracara (*Caracara cheriway*), a member of the Falconidae family. The crested caracara is common throughout the country, and feeds chiefly on carrion, but also eats insects, frogs and snakes.

So, the story of a caracara sitting on a nopal cactus eating a *tuna* has been gradually transformed over time into an eagle sitting on a nopal cactus devouring a serpent.

When Mexico celebrates her official birthday each September, and national symbols are on show everywhere, take a closer look, and remember that perhaps some of the symbols you now see are not quite what most people think!

¡Viva la serpiente! ¡Viva el caracara! ¡Viva México!

19

Huichol Indians preserve traditions

The remote mountains and plateaus of northern Jalisco, extending into the states of Nayarit, Durango and Zacatecas, are home to some 18,000 Huichol Indians. The Huichol heartland straddles the main ridges of the Western Sierra Madre, at elevations of between 1000 and 3000 meters above sea level.

The origins of the Huichol are unclear. Their oral history says they arrived in this area from central Mexico, though most anthropologists believe it is more likely that they came originally either from the north or from the Nayarit coast.

The Huichol, or *Wixárika* ("healers") in their own language, live in scattered, extended family settlements and rely entirely on oral tradition. They are intensely religious and see their time-honored responsibility as protecting all nature's creations. Their shamans perform elaborate ceremonies to a pantheon of gods to ensure bountiful crops, health and prosperity, as well as to preserve nature and heal the Earth.

They view the world as having five regions, corresponding to five mothers: one under the earth and one at each of four cardinal points. The number five is central to many of their beliefs. The sun is carried through the universe by five serpents. The flower of their sacred peyote comes in five colors, as do their cobs of corn: blue, white, reddish purple, yellow and multicolor. The Huichol terms for the five colors of corn are closely associated with the five main points of their cosmos.

The center of the Huichol cosmos—Tee'kata—coincides with the village of Santa Catarina in the Huichol heartland. The typical Huichol home is a simple, one-room dwelling with a thatched roof; some homes have a second room for cooking.

Central to some Huichol ceremonies is peyote, the hallucinogenic cactus they gather during an annual pilgrimage to the eastern cardinal point, the sacred land of Wirikuta, near Real de Catorce in San Luis Potosí. The pilgrimage is an 800-kilometer (500-mile) round trip.

The other cardinal points in Huichol cosmology are the Cerro Gordo mountain in Durango to the north (Huaxa Manaká), Isla del Rey, an island near San Blas, to the west (Tatéi Haramara), and Scorpion Island in Lake Chapala to the south (Xapawiyemeta).

Traditional Huichol handicrafts reflect the importance of the number five. Each of their yarn crosses (often mistakenly referred to as "God's Eyes") is a rhombus, with a center and four corner points, made by wrapping colored yarn around two twigs. Most yarn crosses use several different colors. Compound yarn crosses are made by adding small yarn crosses at each end of the two main supporting twigs, giving five crosses (eyes) in total. Huichol fathers will make a simple yarn cross when a child is born, adding additional crosses annually until the yarn cross is considered complete. This, of course, is assuming that the child survives, given that infant mortality among the Huichol is very high.

The colors used in Huichol artwork also carry lots of symbolism. Blue is taken to mean water or rain and associated with Lake Chapala to the south. Black symbolizes death and is linked to the Pacific Ocean in the west. Red, the color for mother, is usually reserved for sacred places such as Wirikuta in the east. White (clouds) is associated with the north.

Huichol family groups rely on the subsistence farming of corn, beans and squash, which are grown together in a small plot or garden (*coamil*), together with tomatoes, chiles and gourds. Land is cleared by slash and burn, and even steep slopes are cultivated. Meat is rarely eaten except on ceremonial occasions. A few cattle are kept, largely for their value as trade items. They trade in order to acquire other items such as salt, shells, feathers, canned drinks and sandals.

The isolation of the Huichol people has enabled them to retain many of their traditional customs, such as shamans and their annual cycle of ceremonies, but their culture has undergone some significant changes over the past three hundred years.

During colonial times, the Huichol adopted string instruments, the use of metal tools, and the keeping of animals such as sheep, horses and cattle. They also accepted some aspects of Catholic religion.

In the 1950s, government programs financed the first airstrips in the region. Government agencies have since improved roads, opened clinics, and constructed schools for basic education and trades. The government's efforts have included agricultural aid stations, the drilling of wells, and support for the introduction of more modern agricultural techniques and equipment, such as barbed wire and tractors. Other programs have focused on providing alternative sources of revenue such as beekeeping.

All these changes have come at a price. The ancestors of the Huichol practiced a nomadic lifestyle over a large expanse of land in order to acquire the resources they needed for survival. When the Huichol were pushed back into the mountains, they adapted by undertaking an annual migration to gather their sacred peyote. At the same time, they became increasingly dependent on the cultivation of corn. However, in such marginal areas, where rainfall is unreliable, the corn harvest is never guaranteed and in bad years starvation is a real possibility.

Closer links to the outside world have meant that the Huichol can now buy cheap alcohol, and face increased pressure from outsiders who want more grazing land, timber and minerals. This

has also led to the out-migration of many Huichol, either seasonally to work on tobacco plantations in Nayarit or permanently to
nearby cities.

In the past forty years about four thousand Huichol have
become city-dwellers, primarily in Tepic, Guadalajara and Mexico
City. It has also become quite common to see Huichol Indians,
especially the menfolk in their distinctive embroidered clothing,
in tourist-oriented towns, such as San Blas and Puerto Vallarta.

To some extent, it is these city-wise *Huicholes* who have raised
public awareness of their rich culture through the manufacture and
sale of traditional artwork and handicrafts. In addition to embroidered bags and belts, the Huichol make vibrant-colored bead work,
yarn crosses and (more recently) yarn paintings, often depicting
ancient legends. Income from artwork is very variable, but it is an
activity in which women can participate. Unfortunately, trading
in Huichol handicrafts often involves middle men who siphon off
a good portion of the profits, and has also led to a proliferation of
poor quality imitations of Huichol art.

One of the relatively few museum-quality displays of Huichol
Indian work anywhere in Mexico is in the Museo Zacatecano in the
city of Zacatecas. The collection was bought by the state government to prevent it being sold to the University of Colorado. The
185 embroideries on display, as well as many other items, were collected by Dr. Mertens, an American doctor who lived in the mining
town of Bolaños, and offered medical services to the Huichol in
exchange for the occasional gift. Another good place to see high
quality Huichol art is in the store of the small museum alongside
the Basilica de Zapopan in the Guadalajara Metropolitan Area.

Even though the Huichol are one of the most traditional of
all the isolated indigenous groups in Mexico, there is nothing
static about their culture, and it will be interesting to see how it
continues to change in the future.

20

The Tarahumara of the Copper Canyon

In the rugged Copper Canyon region in the north of Mexico live the Tarahumara Indians, renowned for their long-distance running exploits across giant canyons and steep mountain ridges. The people's own name for themselves is *Raramuri*, literally "the light-footed ones" or "footrunners".

The extreme isolation of the Tarahumara, together with their selective adaptation of some elements of outside culture, has enabled them to survive in an extraordinarily hostile natural environment. Today, though, the Tarahumara face numerous challenges as modern life encroaches increasingly on their time-honored traditions.

The Tarahumara also have to manage changes which have been thrust upon them by the government and other agencies trying to help them. So-called modern medicine and education threaten to alter the Tarahumara population balance. Today, more infants survive to adulthood and fewer adults die as a result of accidents. The problem for the Tarahumara is how to feed and support an ever-growing population using existing methods of cultivation and herding.

Their traditional culture reflects their isolation. Tarahumara men and women share roughly equal roles in the local economy, work schedules are flexible and economic specialization is limited.

The Tarahumara have a long-established willingness to share available food whenever necessary in order to ensure survival.

However, this isolation has hindered the emergence of any well-defined leadership system. Lacking an official, political hierarchy makes it much more difficult to resolve disputes. It means that the shy and politically naive Tarahumara have difficulty counteracting intruders, whether they are government officials or drug dealers. As roads in the region are improved, even the most remote sanctuaries of the Tarahumara come under threat.

Some Tarahumara have adopted outside culture far more than others. The great Norwegian ethnologist Carl Lumholtz, when he studied the Tarahumara in the 19th century, recognized the distinction between those he called "gentiles" and the "baptized". The "gentiles" are more traditional and prefer to live in relative isolation; the "baptized" Tarahumara have settled in fixed villages where there is greater influence from outsiders (*mestizos*). Outsiders in this region have tended to occupy the best land by force and then form villages in the European tradition, preserving their economic dominance over the Indians.

Prolonged contact with *mestizos* has led to the gradual transformation of the traditional Tarahumara economic system. Prior to such contacts, the Tarahumara had little or no access to commercially-made alcohol. Their *tesgüino*, a kind of corn beer, took considerable time and effort to make and had to be consumed rapidly, meaning that Tarahumara could get drunk occasionally, but could never remain intoxicated for long. The ready availability of commercial alcohol has completely altered this dynamic.

An innovative project led by women has changed the 3500-inhabitant community of Arareco, eight kilometers from the town of Creel, for the better. Kari Igomari Niwara, a 200-member organization, began in 1992, and is often cited as an outstanding example of what the Tarahumara can do if left to their own devices and given control over their own resources. In this project, Tarahumara women sought encouragement and support, rather than direction and dependence. By 1997 Kari Igomari Niwara had organized a health center, primary school, bilingual literacy program, drinking water system, bakery, three small food supply stores, a handicrafts business, restaurant and collective transportation for the village.

One of the first collective efforts of the Kari Igomari Niwara group was to get the *cantinas* (bars) of Creel closed at 4pm every afternoon, so that their menfolk wouldn't get so drunk. Almost 70 percent of Arareco women had reported being beaten by their husbands, the vast majority of attacks coming when their husbands were drunk. After the initial *cantina* victory, the men became even more repressive, but the women persisted and, four years later, persuaded the church to build them a small health center despite the objections of their local male-dominated council. The women have already reduced nutrition-related infant mortality to a quarter of its former level and have slashed birth rates by half.

Besides the problems brought by ready access to alcohol, several environmental changes, driven by forestry, drug-growing, mining and tourism, have also had adverse impacts on the Tarahumara.

Deforestation in the Copper Canyon region has a long history and has significantly changed the Tarahumara resource base, to the point where their traditional way of life in the canyons is probably impossible to sustain in the future. Deforestation was begun by mining companies, who cut trees for fuel and pit props. In the 1890s the region started to supply timber to the U.S., via concessions given by Chihuahua state governor Enrique Creel to companies such as the Sierra Madre Land and Lumber Company, owned by William Randolph Hearst. Today, many local communal farms (*ejidos*) continue to cut more timber than they replant.

Satellite imagery reveals huge areas that are no longer forested. Soil erosion is rampant. Timber cutting has wrecked many steep slopes, so that there is little chance of reforesting them in the future.

Droughts have exacerbated the problem; their long-term effects go far beyond the obvious. Poor crops in times of drought triggered the abandonment of traditional lands, leading families to become dependent on the sale of handicrafts to tourists, on poorly-paid jobs in the timber industry, or on the cultivation of drugs. Some Tarahumara became the unwilling recipients of blankets and food from charity organizations, others moved to cities like Chihuahua, where they tried to survive by begging.

Forestry required the development of tracks and roads for vehicles. This opened up new areas for mining and tourism. Small stores sprang up, even in remote areas, selling *mestizo* items such as radios, carbonated drinks, cigarettes, and manufactured clothing. Better roads have enabled traders to build a credit relationship with Tarahumara Indians, offering them non-traditional goods in exchange for a share of the next harvest. This has led to problems of indebtedness and exploitation.

The incursion of drug cultivators, growing marijuana and opium poppies in the Canyon country, has further marginalized the *cimarones* ("wild ones"), as the *narcos* call the Tarahumara. Narcotics growers have seized parcels of land by force, and then employed cultivation methods designed for quick results, not sustainability.

Anti-drug policy in this region has gone through several distinct phases. Initially, the emphasis was only on catching those responsible, but then shifted in later phases to various campaigns designed to eradicate the illicit crops. This had a serious environmental downside because aerially-applied herbicides, alleged to include Agent Orange, Napalm and Paraquat, were used widely and indiscriminately.

Drug-trafficking incomers are largely responsible for the incredible, quickly-acquired wealth (and accompanying violence and corruption) that characterizes some settlements on the fringes of the Sierra Tarahumara. In some towns, for example, there are few visible means of economic support but the inhabitants nevertheless drive late-model pickups. Murder rates in these towns are up to seven times the Chihuahua state average, with peaks in May-June and October-November that correspond to planting time and harvest time respectively.

The levels of violence and injustice led Edwin Bustillos (winner of the 1996 Goldman Prize for Ecology) to change the focus of CASMAC (Advisory Council of the Sierra Madre), the NGO he directed, from environmental conservation to the protection of Tarahumara lives. In 1994 CASMAC was instrumental in stopping a $90m-dollar World Bank road-building project that would have opened up still more of the Sierra Tarahumara to timber companies.

Besides deforestation and its resultant impacts, mining has had several other adverse effects on the Tarahumara and the local landscape. Mining activity has increased in the past decade as federal policies encouraged foreign investment in the sector. Mineral extraction has caused a reduction in wildlife and the contamination of water sources, the most damaging pollutants being heavy metals.

Even tourism has brought problems. A $75m plan included improvements to tourist infrastructure, such as highways, runways, drainage systems, water treatment facilities and electricity. The region now has more than sufficient hotels, restaurants and recreational activities for the number of visitors that can get there. Three train stations were remodeled and a tourist cable car was installed. Sadly, the Tarahumara were not consulted. The plan essentially deprived them of some communal land while giving them nothing in exchange.

Occasionally there is some good news. In March 2012, for instance, the Tarahumara won one of the greatest legal victories to date by any indigenous group in Mexico. That was the date when Mexico's Supreme Court recognized that the Tarahumara community of Huetosachi, in Chihuahua, held long-standing indigenous territorial rights, even though they did not formally own all the land. This is truly a landmark victory. The Tarahumara have been guaranteed the right to be consulted over development plans, and to choose the benefits that must be given to them in exchange for any loss of ancestral territory. Finally, the juggernaut of tourism must respect the territories and natural resources of the Tarahumara.

This was David against Goliath. Huetosachi is a tiny settlement of only 16 families, lacking water, electricity or health services, about 10 kilometers from where the main tourist complex was being built near the Divisadero railroad station. Tourist developers are now obligated to create a Regional Consultative Council giving the villagers of Huetosachi and other settlements a say in the negotiations about how development proceeds. This council is expected to include representatives of 27 indigenous communities in the immediate area of Creel and Divisadero.

This landmark court decision could well be the first of many, as indigenous groups elsewhere in Mexico fight their own battles against developers of various kinds. More court cases concerning the Copper Canyon region are likely since it is widely expected that this initial success will lead the Tarahumara to seek compensation for the building of the tourist cable car. The villagers are also reported to be discussing how best to deal with water contamination, which they allege comes from existing hotels, and how best to counter plans to build a golf course on the canyon rim.

21

Train driver sacrificed life for town

The small town of Nacozari (population 13,800) nestles in a valley in the foothills of the Western Sierra Madre (*Sierra Madre Occidental*) in the state of Sonora in northern Mexico.

On 7 November 1907, a young locomotive driver from Nacozari had to make a desperate decision: save his own life or try to save the lives of hundreds in his hometown? He chose the latter, and was driving his dynamite-laden train away from the town when it exploded, killing him instantly. He was only 50 meters from safety. Just 50 meters further, and he could have abandoned the locomotive to its fate and jumped from the burning train to save his own skin.

His actions saved the town. Jesús García became a national hero and, in his honor, 7 November is celebrated each year as Day of the Railroad Worker (*Día del Ferrocarrilero*).

By the end of the 19th century, Nacozari (the name means "abundance of prickly pears") was a lively frontier town of about 5000 people. A worldwide copper boom promised to be the town's path to future wealth. Copper was needed for engines, motors, power plants, telephones, telegraphs, pipes, rods and wire; demand was rising rapidly. Workers flocked in.

In 1895 Nacozari's copper mines were owned by Moctezuma Copper Corporation, a subsidiary of Phelps Dodge. The following year, an important copper reserve was discovered nearby at Pilares. The company enlarged the town: building homes, stores, workshops, warehouses, furnaces and ore concentrators. All the supplies had to be brought in by mule train; most items came from Arizona or California. Ore was packed out of the mines, also by mules.

In 1899 the company built its own eight-kilometer-long narrow-gauge railroad from the mine at Pilares to Nacozari, for easier transport of ore to its concentrators. The elevation difference along this line is considerable, more than 600 meters (2000 feet) from mine to town. Following concentration, the ore was taken to Douglas, Arizona, for smelting. These exports of ore became much easier in 1904 when a standard-gauge railroad line from Agua Prieta was extended to Nacozari.

Jesús García was born on 13 November 1883 in Hermosillo, Sonora. His mother, with her eight children, moved to Nacozari in 1898. García started work with the company railroad as a waterboy, quickly winning promotions to switch man, brakeman, fireman, and finally, by the age of twenty, to engine driver (*maquinista*). His work ethic was so appreciated by his employers that, in 1904, they paid for García and seven of his colleagues to attend the World Fair in St. Louis, Missouri.

García drove locomotive number 2, transporting mineral ore and supplies between the loading yards in the town and the mine. The hazards faced by locomotive drivers included stray donkeys wandering onto the line, saboteurs tearing up the rails, and brake failures. In October 1907 García had managed to halt a train, whose brakes had failed, by reversing the wheels and dumping lots of sand on the line. The train finally ground to a halt only four meters from the end of the line.

García was a popular young man and was engaged to María de Jesús Soqui. He serenaded her regularly, hiring the best local bands each time, and is reported to have done so on the night of Wednesday 6 November 1907.

The following day, García was working as usual and had several return trips scheduled to the mine. The mining company had three locomotives, all made by Porter of Pittsburgh. García operated a 0–6–0 locomotive built to order in 1901. The engines relied on wood for fuel and had to carry copious supplies of water and also sand (to increase the friction between rails and wheels).

When García arrived for work, he was told that he would have to manage without the train's usual conductor, who had been admitted to hospital. By midday, García had completed two trips back from the mine with dozens of loaded ore cars. While other workers tended the engine and loaded the cars for the next trip, García had lunch at his mother's house. Neighbors later confirmed that his mother shared her premonition of doom with him as they ate.

Just after 2.00pm, García set off again toward the mine. Loco-motive number 2 was pulling several cars, the front two of which were open cars containing 70 boxes of dynamite, detonators and fuses. This was strictly against company regulations, which stated that dynamite must be carried only in the rear cars. Other cars that day contained bales of hay.

As they pulled out of the lower yard, stray sparks from the train's chimney stack were blown back onto the first cars, causing a box of dynamite to begin to smolder. Railroad workers aboard the train desperately tried to douse the smoke, but their efforts failed, and the box caught fire.

García realized that if the train exploded near the lower yard, the resulting detonations of the company's dynamite stores and gas tanks would almost certainly destroy most of Nacozari. He also realized that if he jumped from the train, it might run out of steam and roll backwards toward the town before exploding. He ordered everyone else off the train and opened the throttle wide, hoping to put a small ridge between himself and the town, and perhaps reach Camp 6, a secondary loading area en route to the mine. If he could only pass Camp 6, he must have thought, he could safely leap from the train and the train would continue on into uninhabited wilderness.

By 2.20pm García had driven the train six kilometers out of the town and was entering Camp 6 when the cars exploded. García was killed instantly by the massive blast. He died barely a week before his 24th birthday. At least a dozen bystanders were also killed in the resulting carnage. Amazingly, the engine remained on the tracks; it was later sold to the Mereci Southern Railroad of Arizona.

The blast was heard 16 kilometers (10 miles) away. It shattered the glass in many of Nacozari's buildings. Twisted metal was hurled through the air to rain down like shrapnel over a wide area.

But at least García's quick thinking and brave actions had saved the main part of town. Within days, he was being hailed as a hero. Two years after the accident, the town unveiled a permanent memorial to Jesús García, the Hero of Nacozari. Sadly, his fiancée did not live to see this; she died, heartbroken, less than a year after García. On 9 November the state congress decreed that Nacozari would henceforth be known as Nacozari de García. García was declared, posthumously, Hero of Humanity by the American Red Cross. The American Cross of Honor helped fund a memorial in his hometown.

Ten years after the train explosion, García's ashes were reinterred close to his monument in Nacozari. In 1944 the federal government declared that the National Day of the Railroad Worker would be celebrated every 7 November.

Jesús García became a national hero, after whom numerous streets, schools, bridges and parks have been named. There are monuments to him in many towns, including Hermosillo (where the Estadio Héroe de Nacozari was home to the now-defunct Coyotes de Sonora soccer team), Mexico City, Zacatecas, Veracruz, Tapachula, Guadalajara, Mazatlán, Naco, Aguascalientes, Ciudad Obregón, Empalme, San Luis Potosí and Tierra Blanca, as well as in other countries both near (Cuba, Guatemala) and far (United Kingdom, Germany).

Several popular songs or *corridos* were written about him. The best known is "Máquina 501". The composer of this *corrido* took a little poetic license with the engine number. García drove locomotive number 2; 501 was the number of the last locomotive ever operated by the mining company. When it was eventually retired to Nacozari's main square, it was renamed the Jesús García.

Garcia's brave actions have been remembered in a movie, *El Héroe de Nacozari* (1935), directed by Guillermo Calles, and have been the subject of several books, including Kate Tuthill's award-winning *Hero of Nacozari*.

The Moctezuma Copper Co. suspended its operations in Nacozari in 1949, but the discovery of new copper reserves 30 kilometers (20 miles) south-east of the town in 1968 has led to a revival. Mexicana de Cobre, a state-run company, built the infrastructure for modern opencast mining which began in 1980. Eight years later, the mines were bought by a group of investors from Mexico, Canada and Europe.

Nacozari de García has had more than its fair share of economic ups and downs, but remains a pleasant mid-sized town, sustained largely by copper mining and cattle ranching. The town has a population of about 10,000, and is on Highway 17, about 250 kilometers (155 miles) north-east of Hermosillo and 100 kilometers (65 miles) south of Douglas, Arizona.

Archbishop who had miraculous birth

In 1887 Eulogio Gregorio Clemente Gillow y Zavalza (1841–1922) was appointed Bishop of Antequera (Oaxaca) and four years later he became the first Archbishop of Antequera. Named after a town in Spain, Antequera is the Catholic archdiocese of Mexico which includes the city of Oaxaca.

Archbishop Gillow had a somewhat curious background. He was the only child of Thomas Gillow and his second wife. Thomas Gillow (1797–1877), born in Liverpool, England, arrived in Mexico in 1819, when the country was in the throes of the War of Independence (1810–21).

Thomas became a fashionable jeweler and member of elite Mexico City society. His first wife was Soledad Gutierrez de Rivero Martínez de Pinillos, the Marquess of Selva Nevada, a widow who had inherited a large country estate, including the San Antonio Chautla hacienda near the city of Puebla. Soledad already had one daughter, Mara Zavalza y Gutierrez, and a son. Following his marriage, Gillow dedicated himself to running the family estate.

Following his wife's death, Thomas Gillow married her daughter Mara Zavalza. This may have been at least partly in order to resolve legal problems connected to the inheritance of the estate following the death of the Marquess's first husband. Gillow's second marriage was never formally sanctioned by the church. Soon afterwards, Thomas and Mara became the proud parents of Eulogio Gillow.

A wonderful anecdote about Mara is related in the prologue to Joseph Schlarman's *Mexico; A Land of Volcanoes*. In February 1841, about a month prior to giving birth to Eulogio, the Marquess of Selva Nevada collapsed without warning and was taken for dead. Her body, complete with jewels, was placed in a coffin and taken to the Santa Brígida Church in Mexico City. During the night, the sacristan and another individual resolved to steal her jewels. Imagine their surprise when they tried to prise a ring off her finger and she suddenly awoke. She was so startled by finding herself in a coffin, and so fearful that her assailants might kill her, that she offered them a substantial reward for total secrecy. On the eleventh day of the following month, Eulogio was born—a miraculous entry into the world, if ever there was one!

When Eulogio was nine years old, cholera broke out in Puebla. He was rushed to the neighboring city of Tlaxcala, which mercifully escaped the epidemic.

The following year, in 1851, the first World Fair was being held in London. Thomas Gillow took his son to see the fair and then left him in England to go to school. After two years of private coaching, Eulogio entered Stonyhurst College, a famous Catholic private school.

Eulogio continued his education in Europe, with periods of study in Rome, until his return to Mexico, aged 24, in 1865, when he was ordained in Puebla Cathedral; astonishingly he had not seen his father for fourteen years! Sadly, his mother died at sea in 1861 while en route to Europe to visit her son. His mother's death led to renewed legal problems, and Thomas Gillow eventually inherited only the San Antonio hacienda in Chautla.

On Thomas' death in 1877, the hacienda passed to Eulogio who later added an imitation English castle (1898), complete with drawbridge, artificial lakes, and formal, symmetrical gardens, as part of his plans to open an agricultural college. Some of the buildings, including the castle, still stand, and the ex-hacienda's grounds have been restored as a fishing resort, stocked with rainbow trout.

Eulogio Gillow was strongly favored in ecclesiastical and political circles, and became a personal friend of President Díaz. Even so, in 1881, he declined a request to preside over the marriage of Díaz, then 51 years old and a widower, to the president's former English teacher, Carmelita Romero Rubio, still barely 17 years old. Gillow later praised the youthful Carmelita for bringing a more refined and cultured air to Díaz, introducing him to the proper manners of polite society.

Gillow was a man with wide interests. A visiting American anthropologist, Frederick Starr, referred to Gillow as an authority on Mexico's "dwarf races", but Gillow's true passion was promoting modern technology, a love inherited from his father, who had imported the area's first metal plough from England. The plough had worn out so quickly that Gillow senior partnered with a Mr. Marshall to open an iron foundry in Puebla. Marshall went on to make a fortune out of the manufacture and repair of farm and textile equipment. The younger Gillow improved the estate in 1903 by building Latin America's earliest hydro-power plant and introducing electricity.

The estate specialized in wheat and maguey production, and Gillow acquired all kinds of machinery, including a state-of-the-art threshing machine which had won a gold medal in the Philadelphia exhibition of 1876. Sadly, according to another anecdote from *Mexico; A Land of Volcanoes*, the new machine did not work very well and was soon abandoned to rust in a shed. Some years later, the manufacturer of this machine happened to be in a visiting party of tourists. Dismayed that his machine was not in use, he offered to adjust it to ensure that it worked properly. Despite his best efforts, he never did get it to work as intended; the grain produced in Mexico was coarser than that grown north of the border. Monsignor Gillow offered to donate the machine to the Smithsonian Institute, but only on condition that it be exhibited with a large sign reading, "This machine, awarded a gold medal in the Philadelphia exhibition, proved to be entirely useless in Mexico."

As a friend of Díaz, Gillow was an enthusiastic participant in innumerable exhibitions and development projects. He was particularly quick to recognize the potential of the railroad to transform rural Mexico, and increase the profitability of farming. When Gillow was appointed Bishop of Antequera, President Díaz is said to have commented that, "Now, Monsignor Gillow won't leave me in peace until we have a railroad to Oaxaca." Gillow's response was, "Well, Mr President, all hands on deck, when do we begin?" The railroad from Mexico City to Tehuacán and Oaxaca was soon built.

During his time as Archbishop, Gillow restored temples, chapels and churches in the city of Oaxaca, established schools, set up asylums, and was definitely one of the "good guys", even if he was a close friend of Díaz. Gillow was also the model, apparently, for D.H. Lawrence's character Bishop Severn in *The Plumed Serpent* (1926), completed during the English novelist's visit to Oaxaca over the winter of 1924–25.

Without Gillow's efforts, the city of Oaxaca would be but a pale shadow of what it is today. Almost single-handedly, he pushed and prodded until he gained control, one way or another, over the fate of many important religious buildings.

The Santo Domingo convent was only one of the numerous religious buildings in the city to be saved and restored as a result of this Archbishop's extraordinary efforts. The Santo Domingo convent dates back to the 17th century. During the 18th century, it acquired a large collection of works of art, but was repeatedly damaged during the following century, when it was occupied by troops for long periods. In 1869 the destruction of fourteen altarpieces was authorized by state governor Felix Díaz. Looting and neglect combined to cause the loss of countless objects of religious devotion.

In the 1890s, Archbishop Gillow negotiated the recovery of the temple from Porfirio Díaz's troops and immediately began the long process of restoring the temple back to its former glory. Today, this is the jewel in the crown of all Oaxaca's religious architecture—another fortuitous and miraculous rebirth if ever there was one!

Gillow's hacienda was expropriated in 1914 during the Mexican Revolution, and he left Mexico for Los Angeles. Welcomed back to Mexico in 1921, Gillow negotiated the return of a small fraction (150 hectares) of the family estate, which was duly returned to him the following year, shortly before he died on 19 May 1922.

The ex-hacienda of San Antonio Chautla, Mexico's "mini-Versailles", now belongs to the State of Puebla. It is located a short distance north of the main Mexico City-Puebla highway, about 25 kilometers (16 miles) from Puebla, close to San Martín Texmelucan.

23

Cross-dressing maid conned high society

An elaborate tomb in Mexico City's main cemetery, the Panteón Civil de Dolores, is a lasting reminder of one of the nation's strangest ever spoofs. Hand-painted tiles once decorated the tomb depicting Concepción (Conchita) Jurado Martínez as both an elderly grey-haired woman and also as a swanky Spanish businessman, Don Carlos Balmori. Other tiles showed some of the deceptions she carried out.

For many years following her death in 1931, those taken in by her masterful and audacious feats of male impersonation held annual reunions at her grave site. In the words of a 1945 issue of *Time* magazine, the mourners constituted a "society of her worshipful dupes". Today, the grave, and Conchita's exploits, are largely forgotten and most of the tombstone tiles have long since disappeared.

Conchita Jurado was born on 2 August 1865 and relatively little is known about her early life. Was she actually always a charwoman, with aspirations of being an actress, or was she, as some sources claim, really a working actress? Certainly she had a wonderful sense of humor, exemplified by a range of colorful characterizations, even as a child.

Later in life, a bohemian journalist, Eduardo Delhumeau, recognized her talents and helped her hatch the inspired character of Don Carlos Balmori. Over the years, she perfected this party piece and was always ready to assume the appearance, language and behavior of this unbelievably wealthy Spanish gentleman who had poor manners, and whose conversations could be tactless, verging on outrageous.

According to the biography written by a fellow prankster, Conchita first adopted the persona of Carlos Balmori in order to perpetrate a hoax on her father. Balmori, the rich landowner, arrived unannounced, was shown inside, and then begged Conchita's father to give his blessing for him to marry his beautiful daughter. Completely taken in, and taken off guard, the father, shocked, ran Balmori out of the house and then chased him out of the neighborhood. Some time later, disguised as a charcoal seller, Conchita once again tricked her father, this time by insisting on payment in advance of delivery. Her father failed to see through the disguise but refused any payment.

By 1926, now in her 60s and egged on by her friends, Conchita regularly adopted her alter ego and ventured out into high society as wealthy Spanish gentleman Don Carlos Balmori, complete, in the words of *Time*, with "trousers, overcoat, slouch felt hat, a false-diamond stickpin and a false black mustache."

Rumors quickly swirled around "Count" Balmori. He was rich, immensely rich. He had a theater named after him. He was connected, very well connected, to the highest ranks of nobility. Giddy with desire, numerous women fell in love with this eccentric Spanish millionaire, who was also courted by politicians and society grandees.

Conchita had the support of several newspaper editors. According to journalist John Cottrell, Balmori's "financial coups, big-game hunting exploits and amorous adventures around the world were regularly reported, complete with pictures, in the Mexican Press."

Balmori's amazing wealth allowed him to be distastefully blunt and rude about all manner of things. He was able to enjoy high society life for the next five years while perpetrating dozens of elaborate hoaxes, some funny, others positively cruel. He passed away when Conchita died of tuberculosis in a one-room apartment near Mexico City's La Lagunilla market on 27 November 1931.

How were the hoaxes carried out? Balmori developed the knack of promising people exactly what they most wanted, and then backing his promises up with fat checks. In most cases, the recipient was required to undergo some kind of humiliation before financial support was provided. Acceptance of the humiliation revealed their overriding ambition or lack of dignity. Later, when the check turned out to be worthless, the hapless mark was sworn to secrecy and admitted to the exclusive club of the duped, whose members helped plan the next deception.

The club included bankers, generals, musicians, and at least one ex-president. New victims, those chosen to be introduced to Balmori at the next carefully staged party, were known as "new little pigs" (*nuevos puerquitos*). Balmori's "private secretary", Luis Cervantes Morales, later penned a book about the exploits of his master.

During five action-packed years, so many hoaxes were carried out that they even inspired a new colloquialism (not yet found in the Spanish dictionary): *balmoreada*, the kind of social gathering where a Balmori-like joke is played out.

One of the funniest *balmoreadas* ever must have been when Don Carlos held a soiree for friends and asked Valente Quintana, the top detective of the day, to attend because he feared that someone there was actually an imposter. The detective assured the host that he was confident he would spot and unmask the troublemaker long before any mischief took place.

After applying all the tricks of his trade on the guests, he was forced to admit defeat, at which point Don Carlos revealed himself as Conchita, saying, as she always did in the denouement, "Nothing is exactly as it seems to be. Nothing is real. The truth is always hidden." Despite his injured pride, the detective saw the funny side, and subsequently joined the Balmoris in enthusiastically planning further adventures.

Fortunately, the spirit of the *balmoreada* did not die with Conchita's death. Her daring exploits have been remembered in books, poems and songs. Nicaraguan writer Hernán Robleto celebrated her double life in a play entitled *Los millones de don Carlos Balmori* (*The Millions of Carlos Balmori*). Bernard Hilton's 1950 account, "Mexico's deceptive millionaire", was included in *Grand Deception: A selection from the World's Most Spectacular and Ingenious Swindles, Hoaxes & Frauds.*

The last accredited *balmoreada* occurred in 1960. Dr. Luis Cervantes, who during Conchita's life had played the role of Balmori's secretary, asked a well-known but impecunious writer Armando Jiménez (author of *Picardía mexicana*, which sold more than four million copies) to write an account of Conchita's cross-dressing exploits.

Jiménez at first refused, claiming other commitments, but changed his mind when Cervantes promised a ranch he owned as payment. Jiménez checked out the ranch, verified its ownership and lack of outstanding claims, and then turned up at the ranch at the appointed hour to sign the contract in front of a notary. No sooner had he completed the final flourish of his signature than the notary pulled off his moustache, glasses and sideburns, to reveal that he was actually Dr. Cervantes. Dozens of former "victims", many of them renowned artists and intellectuals, then emerged from hiding to celebrate their latest addition with a fun-filled fiesta.

Conchita's refrain every time she revealed the truth—that nothing is ever exactly as it seems to be—is surely one of the most fitting one-liners of all time, and one so perfectly appropriate to many aspects of life in Mexico.

24

Eccentric painter led art revolution

By the time of the Mexican Revolution, which began in 1910, President Porfirio Díaz had been in power for more than 30 years. Artistic expression in Mexico had sunk to an all-time low because painters and sculptors were expected to copy the old masters of Europe, not seek new ways to portray their thoughts and ideas. In the words of famous American art critic Mackinley Helm, "nowhere else in the world, not even in Victorian England, had bad taste in art and decoration been ever so carefully nurtured as in Mexico during the dictatorship of Porfirio Díaz."

In 1910 there were few, if any, signs of the far-reaching revolution in Mexican art which was about to break out: a revolution that would inspire the fine works of Diego Rivera, José Clemente Orozco and David Alfaro Siqueiros, the three greats of Mexico's world-renowned muralists, alongside a host of other painters and sculptors. One of the key figures in this artistic revolution, more or less coincident in time with the country's political revolution, was Gerardo Murillo, better known as Dr. Atl; as an artist, Murillo dropped his birth name in favor of Dr. Atl in the course of his search for a genuinely Mexican identity.

Atl was born in Guadalajara in 1875 and studied at the Guadalajara Boys High School, then located in the building on Calle Liceo that is now the city's Regional Museum. After studying,

briefly, at the Fine Arts Academy in Mexico City, Atl went to Europe, a trip made possible in part by a gift of $1000 from President Díaz himself, to whom Atl had been introduced in 1896.

Europe proved to be a transformative experience. During Atl's stay in Europe, amongst other achievements, he walked from Rome to Paris, and later from Paris to Madrid, won a silver medal in the Salon de Paris for a self-portrait, and found himself increasingly influenced by the impressionist and post-impressionist movements then in vogue in Europe.

Atl returned to Mexico in 1903 full of anti-academic sentiments and convinced that stifled and stuffy Mexican art needed a revolution. He held two surprisingly successful exhibitions in Guadalajara, the first in Tlaquepaque and the second in the garden of the San Francisco church in the city center.

However, Atl's revolutionary beliefs did not endear him to calm, provincial *Tapatios*, as Guadalajara residents are called, and he soon moved back to Mexico City where he became great friends with Joaquin Clausell, later to become Mexico's best known impressionist painter. At the same time, Atl apparently became infatuated with Clausell's 14-year-old niece who, probably fortunately, never reciprocated his feelings!

In 1908, just before the Mexican Revolution began, Atl painted the first modern mural in Mexico, in the San Carlos Academy in Mexico City. The mural—scenes of female nudes—employed Atlcolor, a medium Atl himself had invented for use on a wide variety of surfaces, including plaster, fabric and board. Atlcolors are still manufactured today, enjoying widespread popularity for their relative ease of use.

Atl left Mexico, and the turmoil of the political revolution that followed the resignation of President Díaz, for another trip to Europe. He returned to Mexico in 1914, calling himself Gregorio Stello and wearing the uniform of an Italian Air Force Officer, only days before the outbreak of the first world war. The political situation in Mexico was still very confused, but on his return Atl sided with Venustiano Carranza, an underdog in the power struggle at that time. When the tide turned and Carranza assumed power, Atl was appointed Director of the National Fine Arts Academy, an institution which he promptly closed.

Over the next few years, Atl founded various pro-Carranza newspapers, one of which gave him the chance to employ both Siqueiros and Orozco. During this period, which marked the end of the Mexican Revolution, Atl had several very narrow escapes from death, suffered the ignominy of several short periods of imprisonment, and in general led a full and adventurous life.

By 1921, with the political revolution over, Atl was busy painting murals and writing a landmark book about Mexican Popular Art, in which Tonalá ceramics received great acclaim. He was fast becoming a pillar of the national art scene and had begun a wild, passionate, but short-lived romance with Carmen Mondragón (aka Nahui Olin), an intense relationship punctuated by arguments and violence. Atl would later concede that nymphomaniac Nahui Olin was, among other things, a "green-eyed serpent".

Atl's contribution to the Mexican art revolution had already been considerable; he had encouraged, aided and in several cases taught many major artists of the next generation, including Orozco, Siqueiros, Clausell, Zaraga, Galván and others, including a then unknown Diego Rivera. Atl had pressured his wealthier friends to buy all the works in an exhibition Rivera held to fund a trip to Europe. He had invented Atlcolors, painted several murals (though none have stood the test of time), overseen the rebirth of mural art in Mexico, helped to transform art education throughout the country and made respectable the popular art forms of Mexico such as toys and handicrafts.

A new opportunity suddenly presented itself to Atl in 1943. The eruption of Paricutín volcano in Michoacán in that year led Atl to live on its ever-changing slopes for a year and paint, draw and write to his heart's content. His landscapes took on a distinctive look, much imitated since but never seen before, characterized by bold, heavy lines, simple forms, stark colors and undeniably Mexican in style. Late in his life, Atl borrowed Pemex helicopters and pioneered another entirely new school of landscape painting, "aerial landscapes", painting vast tracts of Central Mexico as seen from above.

The statue of Atl in the stately plaza in front of the Regional Museum in Guadalajara, to one side of the Cathedral, shows Atl at this late stage of his life: bearded, distinguished, but with only one leg. His right leg had been amputated, in a maternity hospital of all places, in 1949 as a result of circulation problems. Atl could still see the humorous side of losing his leg, "I thought I was going to have a baby, but no, they cut off my leg and I left the hospital without a baby and without a leg." His friends attributed his poor circulation to his habit of not changing shoes or socks for months on end, but it was hereditary and compounded by prolonged exposure to the heat and fumes of Paricutín volcano.

A larger-than-life character, even the loss of a leg did not slow him down. Continuing to explore the countryside on mules, he wrote hundreds of pamphlets and continued to pursue his pipe dream of building a super-city for the intellectual and artistic elite. One of the locations Atl considered for this utopian city, which he called Olinka, was Pihuamo in southern Jalisco, where he lived for a year and painted some of his most emotive works. Another of the possible sites was in the Oblatos Canyon, to the north of his native Guadalajara. Today, overlooking the canyon, is the small well-kept Dr. Atl park, established in his honor, with its awe-inspiring view of the Horsetail Waterfall, which Atl had often painted.

Dr. Atl was clearly the inspiration for the fictional artist Professor Arzici in American writer Arthur Davison Ficke's novel, *Mrs Morton of Mexico* (1939). The balding, pipe-smoking, "eccentric but gifted" Arzici is described as "only about eighty years of age", and as "ugly as a goat" with a "long snow-white beard". Both Atl and Arzici were known for their "curvilinear perspective", experimentation with new pigments, and love of painting volcanoes.

Atl's most viewed design today is undoubtedly the Tiffany-made glass curtain of the Bellas Artes opera house in Mexico City.

Gerardo Murillo, Dr. Atl, died in 1964 after 89 years full of intrigue, interest, scandal, notoriety, adventure and eccentricity, and in the middle of teaching himself Chinese. No other single artist had more influence on the Mexican art revolution of the early 20th century that brought so many outstanding Mexican artists to the forefront of world art.

Diego Rivera was absolutely right when he claimed that Atl "was one of the most curious people ever born on the entire American continent".

25

Violinist added notes to musical scale

In 1950 Julián Carrillo, one of Mexico's top violinists, was nominated for the Nobel Prize in physics. The nomination was something of a surprise to the scientific community since Carrillo was far better known as a composer who had invented a microtonal music system known as Sonido 13 (Thirteenth Sound).

His early life was typical of many of the outstanding personalities of the Porfiriato period at the end of the 19th century. Carrillo, the youngest in a family of 19 children, was born in 1875 in Ahualulco, a small town forty kilometers outside the city of San Luis Potosí. He studied music in San Luis Potosí from the age of ten and in 1895 entered the National Conservatory of Music in Mexico City, where he became very interested in the acoustic basis of music and the laws governing the generation of fundamental intervals.

Conventional theory held that when a string is divided by two (for example, by depressing a violin string at its midpoint) the pitch produced will be twice the frequency of the open string, and therefore exactly one octave higher. The interval named a fifth is produced when a string is divided by three, and so on.

On 13 July 1895, after some experimentation, Carrillo found he could depress a violin string so precisely with a razor that he was able to generate sixteen distinct sounds within a single whole tone. This discovery was the basis of Sonido 13.

After four years studying at the National Conservatory, Carrillo had become an outstanding violinist. President Porfirio Díaz was so impressed when he heard him play in 1899 that he gave him a scholarship to Europe, where Carrillo was named one of the first violins in the orchestra of Leipzig Royal Conservatory. During his time in Europe, Carrillo composed his "Sextet in G Major for two violins, two violas and two violoncellos" (1900) and his "First Symphony in D Major for full orchestra" (1901).

In 1904 he won the top award at the Ghent Conservatory International Violin Competition. When Carrillo returned to Mexico, President Díaz presented him with an Amati violin, a gift from the Mexican nation for his excellent performance abroad. Carrillo became a violinist, conductor, composer and teacher at

the National Conservatory but, when the Mexican Revolution wrought havoc on the country, fled to New York City in 1914, following the downfall of Victoriano Huerta's government.

In New York, Carrillo organized and conducted the American Symphony Orchestra and gave a successful performance of his "First Symphony". He also composed the music for David Griffith's film *Intolerance*. It was in New York that Carrillo refined his theory of Sonido 13 (Thirteenth Sound), which became the focus of much of his later life, and which promised to revolutionize classical music. It was called Sonido 13 because Carrillo had 'discovered' the first additional pitch outside the traditional 12 semitones to the octave.

After four years in New York, Carrillo returned to Mexico and for the next six years (1918-1924) was Conductor of the National Symphony Orchestra, which enjoyed great success at this time, and was briefly (1920–21) Principal of the National Conservatory.

After 1920, Carrillo began to popularize Sonido 13, employing intervals smaller than half a tone, as the next stage in the evolution of musical composition. Writing Sonido 13 music required a new notation system and Carrillo devised a numerical notation with 96 divisions to the octave.

Not everyone thought the new microtonal system was an advance. Some of Carrillo's detractors said that it was impossible for the human ear to perceive such small intervals, while others argued that he must have stolen the idea from Europe.

The first major Sonido 13 concert took place on 15 February 1925 in the Teatro Principal in Mexico City, with a program of compositions by Carrillo and several of his students using quarters, eighths, and sixteenths of a tone, performed on specially adapted instruments. In December 1925 Carrillo took Sonido 13 to Havana, Cuba. The following year, he was invited to New York where the League of Composers commissioned him to write a microtonal work. His "Sonata casi fantasia in quarters, eighths and sixteenths of a tone" was first performed at the New York Town Hall on 13

March 1926. Afterwards, Leopold Stokowski commissioned a second work, the "Concertino in quarters, eighths and sixteenths of a tone", which he performed with the Philadelphia Symphony Orchestra in New York and Philadelphia.

In 1930 Carrillo organized the world's first Thirteenth Sound Symphony Orchestra, in which all the musical instruments could play microtones. This orchestra performed from 1930 to 1931, always conducted by either Carrillo or Stokowski.

During the latter part of his life, Carrillo wrote widely about Sonido 13, while continuing to develop the appropriate instruments to play microtonal music. In 1940 he applied for patents for a set of fifteen metamorphoser pianos, capable of producing, respectively, complete tones, thirds of a tone, quarters, fifths, sixths, sevenths, eighths, ninths, tenths, elevenths, twelfths, thirteenths, fourteenths, fifteenths, and sixteenths of a tone! Each piano had 96 keys, the same number as a regular piano, but the span in octaves of each piano depended on the fractions of a tone it was designed for. Hence, the piano for quarters of a tone covered four full octaves, while the piano for sixteenths of a tone covered only one octave! In 1949 the first metamorphoser piano (for thirds of a tone) was made, and the following year Carrillo took it to the Paris Musical Conservatory. The complete set of fifteen metamorphoser pianos won a Gold Medal at the 1958 Brussels' World Fair.

Back in the U.S., in Pittsburgh in 1950, Leopold Stokowski conducted the first performance of "Horizons: Symphonic Poem for violin, cello and harp in quarter, eighths and sixteenths of a tone", with further performances in Washington, D.C., Baltimore and Minneapolis.

Carrillo received numerous awards during his lifetime, including the Legion of Honor from France and the Great Cross of Merit from Germany. In Mexico, the government of his native state of San Luis Potosí declared 13 July (the anniversary of Carrillo's 1895 experiment) a state holiday in his honor and renamed his birthplace as Ahualulco del Sonido 13.

However, perhaps the most surprising nomination Carrillo ever received was for the Nobel Prize in physics. This resulted from experiments he made in New York University in 1947, when he proved that the conventionally accepted "node's law" had to be rectified, and that the frequency of the note produced by halving the length of a string is actually slightly more than twice the frequency of the base note. The Nobel prize that year was eventually awarded to Englishman Cecil Frank Powell who had developed a photographic method of studying nuclear processes.

The *Times* of London summed up Carrillo's contribution to music as follows: "Carrillo devoted his life to scrutinize an unsuspected microtonal world, undoing and rebuilding our chromatic musical scale. Even if we feel tempted to call him the disintegrator of the musical atom, this name does not do justice to the wonderful emotional world he has discovered. His is the greatest and the most surprising musical revolution since Terpander, the Greek musician, added two notes to the Chinese pentaphonic scale twenty six centuries ago."

The inventor of Sonido 13 died in Mexico City on 9 September 1965. Various streets, schools and institutions have been named in his honor. They include a residential neighborhood and Youth Symphony Orchestra in San Luis Potosí, the Avenida Julián Carrillo in the city of Chihuahua, at least two streets, a radio station and two schools in Mexico City (where there is also a Calle Sonido 13), and the municipal auditorium in Apan, Hidalgo.

Long live the Thirteenth Sound! *¡Viva el Sonido 13!*

26

January's weather foretells year ahead

Many Mexicans, especially peasant farmers or *campesinos*, who are closer to the land than most, believe that the weather during the month of January serves as a long-range forecast for the entire year. The precise prediction system is thought to be based on long cycles of observations carried out in an age when people depended far more on the weather than they do today. The system is quite complicated.

The first twelve days of January are known as *las cabañuelas "a derechas"*. The weather on 1 January foretells the likely weather for the rest of the month. The weather on 2 January predicts the weather for February and so on, with the weather of 12 January suggesting likely conditions for December. The next twelve days (13 to 24 January inclusive) are known as *las cabañuelas "a rataculas"*. This time, the weather of 13 January foretells December, that of the following day November, and so on.

Next, each of the six days from 25 January to 30 January inclusive is divided at noon. The morning of 25 January represents January, the afternoon February. The morning of 26 January hints at March's weather, while the afternoon applies to April's, and so on.

Finally, even the 24 hours of 31 January are used. Each hour in the morning will be reflected in the weather from January to December. Presumably the weather from midnight to 1.00am is a true reflection of what has already happened in January! Then, each hour in the afternoon can be used to forecast future weather in the reverse direction. Hence, noon to 1.00pm gives us clues for December, 1.00 to 2.00pm for November and so on. Apparently, an alternative version, used in some parts of northern Mexico, divides 31 January into 12 periods of two hours each, with each division corresponding to the months in reverse order.

Whatever the details, the system is said to be at least as reliable as scientific forecasts over the same time period. Though, thinking about it, perhaps that is not very hard!

The same *cabañuelas* system is used in various parts of Spain, but the annual forecast does not always begin on the same day. For instance, in Alcozar, *las cabañuelas "a derechas"* begin on 13 December. Elsewhere in Spain, they start on 2 August or 13 August. According to Divina Aparicio de Andrés, predictions in Alcozar based on *las cabañuelas* lasted until well into the 1940s, but their use has declined since.

The historical origins of the word *cabañuelas* are unclear. Some sources claim that the system's roots lie in the Old World, and go back to well before the Spanish colonization of the New World. Writing in *Mexico Desconocido*, Homero Adame asserts that the origins date back to the Zumac, or "Festival of Luck", in the Babylonian calendar. The term *cabañuelas* may be connected to the Hebrew version, which was the "Festival of the Tabernacles". Adame also points out that twelve days in the middle of winter were used in India to forecast the future weather conditions. He applies the lore of *las cabañuelas* to the weather experienced in the city of San Luis Potosí in 2001, finding that it does a fairly good, though not perfect, job of predicting the weather later in the year.

However, an alternative viewpoint is argued by Graciela Minaya in an article originally published in 1945 in *La Nación*, a Mexico City daily. She views *las cabañuelas* as an example of the common heritage of the ancient indigenous peoples of Mexico, central America, and the larger Caribbean islands that was passed down from one generation to the next. This would explain the variability in details from one country to another.

In her view *las cabañuelas* were probably handed down from the Maya. The Maya calendar had 18 months, each of 20 days, followed by five additional "non-month" days. The Maya version of *las cabañuelas* used the first 18 days of the first month to predict the weather for the 18 months of the year. To complete the system, the 19th day of the first month predicted the weather for the summer solstice, and the 20th the weather for the winter solstice.

The Maya version was known as *Chac-chac*. For those who are curious, the 18 months are: *pop, uo, zip, zots, tzec, xul, yakin, mol, chen, yax, zac, ceh, mac, kankin, muan, pax, kayab, cumhú*. The spare 5 days are known as *uayeb*. The days of each month went in the following order: *ik, akbal, kan, chiechán, cimí, manik, lamat, muluc, oe, chuen, eb, bon, ix, men, cíb, cabán, eznab, cauac, ahua, imix*. Minaya argued that the 16th day, *cabán*, gave rise to the word *cabañuelas*, presumably because it had some additional significance, perhaps in terms of some other calendric calculation or time marker.

The testimony of Román Pané, a monk of the order of St. Geronimo, who accompanied Columbus on his second voyage, lends credence to the idea that *las cabañuelas* originated in the New World. While in Haiti, Pané recorded the fact that "these Indians know by consulting their gods and observing the first days of the year which days will be good, which will be bad, which will be rainy and which dry." Pané, incidentally, is thought to have been the first person to take tobacco back to Spain.

How did the Maya come up with such a system in the first place? They had already undertaken sophisticated astronomical observations and had developed advanced mathematical and calendric systems, even to the point of being able to predict the arrival of some comets. So, perhaps by long and patient observation of their weather patterns, they had also amassed evidence of cyclical weather trends.

Whatever their origin, *las cabañuelas* give us an opportunity each year to record the weather and test if they really still work.

If you happen to be traveling in Mexico in January, listen carefully. If, say, the 8th of the month turns out to be cloudy and rainy, you may hear someone exclaim, "*¡Ay! es que estamos en la cabañuela de agosto*". (We are in the August cabañuela). You'll know exactly what they mean, and make both Chac, the Maya rain god, and Kukulcan, the Maya wind god, proud.

27

World's most popular romantic song?

Consuelo Velázquez was one of Mexico's best-known modern songwriters. She wrote her most famous song—"Bésame mucho"—before she was 20 years old. When asked, years later, whose love had inspired the powerful lyrics, she replied that she had written it before she had ever been kissed but when she longed for that day to come, and that the entire song was based purely on her imagination.

Quite some imagination! The song has been translated into more than 20 languages, and been sung in many different styles, by dozens of artists ranging from The Beatles, Frank Sinatra, Sammy Davis Jr. and Plácido Domingo to Pedro Vargas, Linda Rondstadt, Diana Krall, Elvis Presley and Mexican heartthrob Luis Miguel.

Consuelo Velázquez Torres Ortiz was born in Ciudad Guzmán, Jalisco, on 21 August 1920 (some biographers claim 1916), but grew up in Guadalajara. She began playing piano when she was four, gave her first public recital at age six at the local Academia de Serratos, and moved to Mexico City in her teens to attend the National Conservatory at the Palace of Fine Arts. She became a concert pianist in 1938, and honed her skills in a workshop given by Claudio Arrau, who praised her talent.

Velázquez had already written several popular songs, saying they came from her heart, before she took a job overseeing classical

music programs for the pioneering radio station XEQ. The station's announcers introduced her as a "prestigious European musician with a complicated Polish surname". Velázquez went along with this subterfuge and began to introduce her own compositions into the show, attributing their authorship to an imaginary friend since it was not considered seemly at the time for a serious concert pianist to lower themselves to compose popular bolero songs.

Listeners, however, knew what they wanted, and demanded more boleros and less classical music. The station manager, Mariano Rivera Conde, begged Velázquez to reveal the real name of her friend, so that he could be sure copyright law was being upheld. Velázquez admitted her deception, which did nothing to stop the increasing popularity of her songs at a time when news programs were full of the events of the Second World War. On 25 October 1944, six years after they first met, Velázquez married Rivera; the couple later had two sons.

The original Spanish-language lyrics of "Bésame mucho" are direct and urgent: Bésame, bésame mucho, / Como si fuera esta noche la última vez ("Kiss me, kiss me a lot, / as if tonight were the last time"). The usual English lyrics take some poetic license with the original to exaggerate the intent: "Bésame, bésame mucho, / Each time I cling to your kiss, I hear music divine"

The melody of "Bésame mucho" was inspired by the piano piece "Quejas, o la Maja y el Ruiseñor" ("Plaints, or the Maiden and the Nightingale"), composed by Spanish musician Enrique Granados for his 1916 opera *Goyescas*.

The first recording of "Bésame mucho" was in 1941 by Emilio Tuero and Chela Campos; the song became a huge Big Band hit during the Second World War. At one point it topped the U.S. hit parade for 12 straight weeks, the only Mexican song ever to do so. In 1999 "Bésame mucho", the most sung and recorded Mexican song in the world, was declared "Song of the Century" at a Univisión event in Miami, Florida. That same year, Velázquez was invited to Puerto Rico to receive the Grandeza de la Mujer Latina award.

"Bésame mucho" featured in numerous movies, including *A toda máquina* (1951), *The moon over Parador* (1988), *Sueños de Arizona* (1993), and *Moskva Slezam ne Verit* ("Moscow does not believe in tears"), a Russian movie which won the 1980 Oscar for Best Foreign Film. More recently, the song is heard several times during Alfonso Cuarón's 1998 romantic drama *Grandes esperanzas* ("Great expectations").

"Bésame mucho" brought fame and numerous awards to Consuelo Velázquez, including an award from the Consejo Panamericano de la Compositores and a Special Citation of Achievement Award from the U.S. Broadcast Music Incorporated (BMI). Invited to Hollywood to meet the legendary Walt Disney, she found him to be "nice, kind and respectful." Velázquez agreed to work on Disney's *The Three Caballeros*. During the filming of this movie, Rita Hayworth stopped by and insisted on meeting and being photographed with Velázquez, as did Esther Williams, Orson Welles, Errol Flynn, Clark Gable and many others. Velázquez, though, turned her back on Hollywood, and headed back to Mexico to marry her sweetheart.

According to her close friends, Consuelo Velázquez remained a gentle, humble person throughout her life, often telling anecdotes about her life as if she was talking about someone else. She continued to play the piano most afternoons until well into her 80s.

Among other songs she wrote that were popular in their day are "Yo no fui" (sung most famously by Pedro Infante, but also by Pedro Fernández), "Anoche", "Al nacer este día", "Aunque tengas razón", "Déjame quererte", "Pensará en mí", "Amar y vivir", "Que seas feliz" (interpreted by Luis Miguel in his album *México en la piel*), "No me pidas nunca", "Volverás a mí", "Chiqui" and "Cachito". The last two named were dedicated to her two sons.

Velázquez composed more than forty songs in total, and at the time of her death had just finished three more: "Mi bello Mazatlán", the romantic, blues-style song "Donde siempre" and "Por el camino", written especially for Luis Miguel's next album.

She served as president of the Mexican Society of Authors and Composers, and was also vice-president of The International Confederation of Authors and Composers Societies which now has members from 120 countries.

In 2012 Google celebrated what would have been her 92nd birthday with a Google doodle on its Mexican search page depicting a soldier kissing his loved one goodbye as he left for the war.

Consuelo Velázquez, "Consuelito", can rightfully be considered Mexico's greatest female composer ever. Her life and her songs will be remembered with affection by music lovers everywhere for years to come. Her impact spanned the world. Consuelo Velázquez, songwriter extraordinaire, died on 22 January 2005, at the age of 84.

Que descansa en paz—May she rest in peace.

28

Mexico's soundscapes and traffic whistles

Mexico's urban soundscapes are among the most distinctive on the planet. Four notes on a pan flute signify that the knife sharpener is nearby, a ringing hand bell alerts home owners that the garbage truck is in the street, and the clanging of gas tanks means that the gas truck is in the neighborhood. During Mexico's National Sound Week in 2010, special "sound walks" were arranged in several major cities, guiding participants along routes featuring a variety of typical local sounds.

In Mexico City, one of the more unusual soundscapes is heard at Plaza Santo Domingo, a downtown square where the rapid clickety-clack of manual typewriters echoes from surrounding arcades as public typists quickly fill out government forms and write letters for people lacking essential literacy skills. With rising literacy and computers, the days of these scribes and their vintage typewriters are numbered.

Also on the decline is the small army of cobblers once found in every city, whose tap-tap-tapping of small nails breathed new life into tired footwear, sparing owners the expense and discomfort of new shoes. Equally, some longtime residents will be saddened at the gradual demise of the nerve-tingling, out-of-tune barrel organs that used to roam the streets and were a frequent distraction from daily life.

Some parts of Mexico rely more on whistles than others. One particular indigenous group in Oaxaca, the Chinantec, are fluent in one of the most curious of all the dozens of indigenous languages still spoken in Mexico. Their conventional spoken language is complemented by a language based entirely on a very complex system of intricate whistles. Only a few people remain who speak this whistled language fluently. The language is whistled primarily by men and it is believed to have developed to allow communication between isolated settlements that were too remote from one another for conventional spoken language to be effective. The Chinantec's whistled language has three distinct subsets, designed to be used over different distances, with the loudest enabling them to communicate effectively over distances of around 200 meters (650 feet).

The Chinantec whistled language is now largely confined to the misty, fog-shrouded slopes of the Sierra Juárez in the northern part of Oaxaca state, a region where high rainfall totals support luxuriant vegetation. Dr. Mark Sicoli, Assistant Professor of Linguistics at Georgetown University, has conducted extensive fieldwork in the area and believes that the astonishing whistled language of the Chinantec should be included on the lengthy list of Mexico's endangered cultural wonders.

Sounds and whistles may be very useful means of communication, but prolonged exposure to environmental noise can have deleterious effects on an individual's well-being. Mexico, like many countries, has enacted legislation to limit people's exposure to loud noise on the grounds that such exposure can seriously damage health, resulting in lost working days and increased healthcare costs.

Mexico's official noise norm, first published in 1995, follows World Health Organization guidelines. The technical details were modified in 2013, establishing maximum permitted noise levels in a variety of different settings. For example, the maximum noise outside a residence may not exceed 50 decibels between the hours of 10.00pm and 6.00am. Note, though, that these limits apply to fixed sources of noise, not to the occasional passing vehicle with loudspeaker blaring!

In urban areas, traffic noise and accompanying police whistles and sirens are sufficient to drive many visitors to despair. Mayhem prevails in many Mexican cities during rush hours. The traffic in some big cities rarely seems to let up, or slow down, as vehicles jockey for the best position before becoming ensnarled in a tangled web of blocked intersections and jam-packed avenues.

Even thirty years ago, a standing joke (pun intended) in Mexico City was that the city's largest parking lot was actually the ring road or *periférico*. Built originally as a means of diverting traffic away from the downtown areas, the periférico (much of it six lanes wide in each direction) was swallowed up in the 1960s and 1970s as the city's boundaries pushed inexorably further and further into the state of Mexico. The *periférico* no longer helped drivers escape the clutches of Mexico City's traffic; it actively ensured that many would get entrapped in it with no easy means of escape.

A casual observer of the traffic flows in most large Mexican cities could easily be forgiven for thinking that the entire experience is one best described as out-of-control anarchy. But, amazingly, some parts of the apparently chaotic daily movement of tens of thousands of vehicles between home and workplace are very carefully choreographed by traffic signs and police officials.

While most road signs, traffic signals and police gestures are self-evident, and unlikely to cause much confusion, there are some which newcomers may find difficult to interpret correctly.

To help drivers out, traffic-direction gestures by police are usually accompanied by penetrating whistles. These *toques de silbato* are delivered with wonderful overstatement by many traffic policemen, making them fully paid-up members of the Guild of Street Entertainers. It was several years before I discovered that these seemingly incessant whistles actually had very specific and well-defined meanings.

In Mexico City and the state of Mexico, a single short whistle means "Stop!", while two short whistles means "Carry on!"

A single long whistle, however, means "Everyone stop!" Newcomers should be advised that the difference between one short and one long whistle may only become apparent to you when the vehicle immediately in front screeches to a complete and totally unexpected halt.

This system sounds simple enough but, like so many facets of Mexico, it is not quite as straightforward as it first appears. Almost all traffic regulations are local (municipal) or state, not federal, rules. The fine print of traffic statutes therefore varies from one place to the next. The precise body positions used by the police when giving hand gestures (at least those used in directing traffic), as well as the number, length and meaning of whistles, are all defined in each state's traffic regulations.

Almost all states agree that one short whistle means "Stop!", while two short whistles still means "Carry on!" For other indications, though, the airwaves are somewhat more confused.

For instance, in the states of Guanajuato and Nuevo León, three or more short whistles means "Speed up!" This is deceptively similar to the situation in Jalisco, where four short whistles means "Speed up!" However, in Jalisco, you'd better be aware that three "regular length" (i.e. neither long nor short) whistles are actually an indication for "All traffic to stop!" Newcomers who slam their brakes on when they hear three normal whistles in Guadalajara should therefore check in their rear-view mirror in case they are being tailgated by a vehicle with Guanajuato or Nuevo León plates, whose driver may already be pressing his or her foot down hard on the accelerator instead of the brake.

Making matters even more complicated, while a single long whistle in Mexico City means "Everyone stop!", in Jalisco, it officially means "Take care!" or "Proceed with caution!"

Next time you're caught in rush hour, or hopelessly lost while trying to navigate through an unfamiliar city, listen carefully and make every effort to avoid infringing, even accidentally, any of the many sound (pun intended) commands issued by traffic officials.

Does all this mean that driving in Mexico is safer than in most places? Not really. According to the latest available data, there are about 21 traffic fatalities a year in Mexico for every 100,000 people. This is roughly the same rate as in Brazil (18), China (17), India (17), Peru (22), Venezuela (22), Russia (25), and Pakistan (25) but well behind Japan (5), U.K. (5), Germany (6), Canada (9) and the U.S. (11). Traffic accidents are currently the leading cause of death for those aged 5-35 in Mexico, and the second cause of permanent injury for all ages.

So, wherever you go, drive safely and remember, as Mexico's road safety campaigns exhorted years ago, "Your children are waiting for you" and "Better late than never!"

29

Sports fans embrace Mexican wave

The Mexican wave (*La Ola*) is the rippling wave effect that passes right around a stadium full of spectators when the spectators stand up in turn, arms raised, and then sit down again with their arms lowered. Now common at sports events and concerts, this cooperative, coordinated and spectacular sight gained popularity after the 1986 World Cup soccer competition held in Mexico.

The historical origins of this seemingly spontaneous social ritual are disputed, but it certainly predates the 1986 World Cup and was originally called either the "human wave", or simply "the wave", rather than the Mexican wave. Numerous independent claims have been made as to where it was first orchestrated. The rival claims include those of the fans of the Seattle Mariners baseball team; the "yell-leader" Rob Weller and marching band director Bill Bissell of the University of Washington's "Huskies" American football team; and "Krazy" George Henderson at a Major League baseball game in 1981. Canadians argue for the wave being invented at an Edmonton Oilers ice hockey game in 1980.

Whoever started it, the wave was certainly widely practiced in the early 1980s at American and Canadian football games.

Many Mexicans prefer the (as yet unsubstantiated) version, advanced by Alan López in a comment on the website of the U.K.'s *Guardian* newspaper, that the first wave was performed during the half-time break by fans watching a local derby soccer match between Monterrey (Club de Fútbol Monterrey) and Tigres (Club de Fútbol Tigres de la Universidad Autónoma de Nuevo León) in the city of Monterrey, Mexico, in the 1970s. However, the Tigres' own website claims that the first wave was held at its stadium on 18 September 1984 during a friendly game between Mexico and Argentina that ended in a 1-1 draw.

Irrespective of its geographic origin, the wave's rise to prominence on the world stage came in Mexico during the World Cup finals in 1986. I can personally vouch for the fact that it was regularly performed in Mexico City's main stadium, the Estadio Azteca, during this competition, since I was one of the thousands of enthusiastic participants. *La Ola*, not surprisingly, received extensive television coverage. The persuasive power of television ensured that the term Mexican wave soon entered the vernacular vocabulary, to describe an end-of-the-20th-century phenomenon that has transformed how spectators react in sports stadia around the globe.

It may not be clear when, or where, the Mexican wave originated, but the origin of each individual wave event is now much better understood as a result of some pioneering mathematical modeling performed by a team of two biological physicists from Hungary, together with an economics and traffic researcher from Germany. They co-wrote the article, "Mexican waves in an excitable medium", published in *Nature* in September 2002. A supporting web page, still working in 2016, includes a video clip and animated graphic showing a typical Mexican wave. It also features fascinating interactive graphics to show how various mathematical variables affect the probability, form, and speed of travel of Mexican waves in a hypothetical sports stadium.

In physics terminology, the Mexican wave is an example of a transverse wave: the spectators move only vertically (standing up and then sitting down again) but the wave form travels horizontally around the stadium. The researchers studied video footage of fourteen wave events at large stadiums and built a mathematical model that mimics their development and subsequent movement, similar to the models used for predicting the movements of heart tissue or a forest fire.

They found that three out of every four waves travel clockwise around the stadium (perhaps because the majority of people are right-handed) and that they typically move about 12 meters (20 seats) a second. Interestingly, it requires only 30 or so fans standing up simultaneously to start the ripple effect leading to a fully-fledged wave. The success of the computer models means that future studies may lead to methods of predicting how unrest will spread in an excited crowd and therefore suggest precisely how security personnel can best keep tense situations under control.

So, we now know that you only need a small core group of fans to start a wave. But, how many people do you need to break the official Guinness record for the world's longest Mexican wave? Well, surprisingly, until November 2002, the official record (for a single line wave) stood at only 3276. By November 2002 this had risen to 5805, the number of people who lined Aberavon Beach near Port Talbot in South Wales a few months earlier. As of early 2016, according to the Guinness Records website, the longest Mexican wave line had 8453 participants and had been organized by Realizar Impact Marketing at the Parque das Nações in Lisbon, Portugal, on 12 August 2007.

Of course, the longest wave is certainly not the largest wave. Even back in 1986, figures like 5000 were easily exceeded, by at least a factor of ten, on numerous occasions during the 1986 World Cup. In July 2002 more than 250,000 spectators lined the 40-kilometer-long (25-mile-long) route through the streets of Mexico City that was traveled by Pope John Paul II when he visited the city. They attempted the largest (and longest) wave in history, but this seems never to have been ratified by Guinness. As of 2016, the Guinness Records website lists the largest Mexican wave in terms of the number of people as the 157,574 wave participants at

Bristol Motor Speedway during the Sharpie 500 NASCAR Sprint Cup Series race in Bristol, Tennessee, on 23 August 2008. The website gives the longest Mexican wave, in terms of time (lasting 17 minutes 14 seconds) to the musical group Tube and more than two thousand fans in Hanshin Koshien Stadium in Nishinomiya, Japan, on 23 September 2015.

Some of these waves should perhaps not be considered genuine Mexican waves, given that the dictionary definition involves spectators in a stadium! In any event, believe me, it's much more exciting to see a Mexican wave racing several times around a packed and noisy soccer stadium than swishing tamely along an otherwise deserted beach.

Mexican wave has now become a term used in many other contexts besides the crowd behavior phenomenon described in this article. For example, molecular enzymologists have used it to describe the characteristic motion in a "Model for ssDNA translocation" (whatever that is). Mexican Wave is also a type of acrylic yarn, manufactured in several variegated patterns, that can be machine-washed, laid flat to dry, and is considered excellent value for money!

The term has also been applied to "shimmering", the arching movements that thousands of bees make with their bodies in a packed hive to transmit information from one part of the hive to another and warn off would-be predators.

For a solo Mexican wave, where thousands of friends are not necessary, consider looking at YouTube and perfecting the facial gymnastics to create your own eyebrow Mexican wave.

Whenever, wherever and however you next participate in a Mexican wave, have fun!

30

Mexican cats have only seven lives?

While some Anglo beliefs, such as walking under a ladder being unlucky, are essentially the same in Mexico, many other Anglo sayings and superstitions are subtly different once you cross the border into Mexico.

For starters, consider your pet cat. In English-speaking countries, cats are considered to have nine lives. In Mexico, however, cats have only seven lives (*siete vidas*). Perhaps they used up two lives as kittens just getting to be old enough to be a cat? Or perhaps the difference reflects the differences in the human lifespans in the two cultures? The life expectancy of someone born in the U.S. in 2014 was 77.1 years for men and 81.9 years for women, compared with 72.7 years and 78.3 years respectively for people born in Mexico.

Still on the subject of luck, should you ever break a mirror, then hope that this happens in Mexico, rather than elsewhere. In the U.S. and Canada the superstition is that breaking a mirror will bring you seven years of bad luck, and there is little you can do about it. However, in Mexico the belief is that if you act quickly and carefully collect all the broken pieces and place them in a bowl of water for at least 24 hours, then you can safely throw them away without lasting harm—excluding the possibility of cut fingers, obviously. The bad luck superstition may have arisen in ancient times from when fortunes were sometimes told by looking in a bowl of

water, with the seer so shocked if the bowl was ever upturned as to be convinced that serious bad luck would surely follow. In pre–Columbian times the native peoples in Mexico utilized polished metals or, in some cases, the black, glassy, volcanic rock obsidian as mirrors, all of which were much more difficult to break.

Staying on the subject of luck, it is not Friday the thirteenth that is considered an unlucky day in Mexico but Tuesday the 13th (*martes trece*). Perhaps that is just as well since it means that it can never simultaneously be unlucky in all three North American countries. Hence, on days when it is unlucky to do business in the U.S. and Canada, it will not be so in Mexico and vice versa. Language and history may help explain why Mexicans are careful every Tuesday the thirteenth. The number thirteen is unlucky in several cultures. Tuesday in Spanish is martes, derived from Mars, the Roman god of war, and Tuesday the thirteenth happens to coincide historically with the fall of Constantinople during the Fourth Crusade (13 April 1204); maybe some people have long memories.

Continuing on a calendric note, how about the first day of April, also known in the English-speaking world as April Fool's Day or All Fool's Day? Anyone playing minor pranks on someone on this day in Mexico is likely to be met with blank stares, or looks of shock or horror, depending on the prank. The Mexican equivalent comes much later in the year, on 28 December, Day of the Holy Innocents (*Día de los Santos Inocentes*). This is when Mexican children will borrow, with no intention of repaying, small trinkets or sums of money from unsuspecting friends and relatives whom they consider a soft touch. Once they've received the loan, they say the following verse, or something along similar lines:

Inocente Palomita	Innocent little dove
Que te dejaste engañar	You have let yourself be fooled
Sabiendo que en este día	Knowing that on this day
Nada se debe prestar.	You should lend nothing.

So, be careful on 28 December if anyone admires your most prized possessions!

Danger lurks in all societies, but how do you know danger is at hand? In English, a variety of warning shouts are commonly used to warn others of danger, depending on the situation. For example, "Below!" is used by climbers when rocks are dislodged and could fall on someone climbing behind them. "Behind you!" is the pantomime shout that alerts you to danger from behind, and so on. The Mexican equivalent, when dangerous situations occur and someone wants to warn others, is a shout of "*¡Aguas!*", often repeated several times. What does "Waters!" have to do with danger? It hardly sounds like the best way to inform non-Spanish speakers that danger lurks. However, it has a perfectly logical origin.

Before towns and cities had any kind of public sewage (drainage) systems, sewage was simply thrown into the street where the stench often became unbearable. "*¡Aguas!*" was the shout used to warn passers-by in the street below that the contents of "night buckets" were about to be emptied onto their heads. In consequence, "*¡Aguas!*" is still commonly used in Mexico for "Danger!", "Look out!", or "Heads up!", in many different contexts.

In Mexico, there are, in addition, any number of sayings and superstitions that have no direct equivalent in English. The following sayings are commonly passed on from one generation to the next in Mexican families:

"Never do cold things while hot, or hot things while cold." This explains why your home-help will not do any ironing immediately after mopping the floors. It is believed that the sudden change of temperature can cause rheumatism.

Perhaps it is different now that everyone is glued to their computer screens but, decades ago, many Mexicans would say that coming out of a cinema without rubbing your eyes could lead to blindness.

"Go outside with your luggage on New Year's and you'll travel the world."

"Don't let anyone sweep your feet or you'll forever be single."

"If you scratch your itchy palm, money won't come your way." If your palms itch, then it is better to slip your hand inside your pocket since itching palms means money is coming, and that's where money should go.

"If you drop a tortilla on the floor, a large number of visitors (or, in some variants, in-laws) will visit."

"Cutting a baby's fingernails before the child's first birthday can cause severe vision problems."

"Don't let anyone pass you a saltshaker by placing it directly into your hand, or you will have bad luck; they should place the saltshaker on the table within your reach."

Among the Mexican proverbs quoted in Jeff M. Sellers's delightfully-illustrated *Folk Wisdom of Mexico* are the following:

"*Para tonto no se estudia.*" (One needn't study to become a fool).

"*No hagas hoy lo que puedas hacer mañana*" (Don't do today what you can put off until tomorrow).

"*Todo el rato que esté enojado, pierde de estar contento*" (All time spent angry is time lost being happy).

"*De médico, poeta, músico y loco todos tenemos un poco*" (Of doctor and poet, musician and madman we each have a trace).

Even in death it is impossible to escape folk beliefs. In the old days, when a death occurred, a bucket of vinegar would often be placed beneath the coffin or bed on which the body lay, in order to collect any cancers leaving the body. Otherwise, any visitor with a wound or broken skin who entered the room would be at risk of catching them.

It is precisely these sayings, superstitions and subtle differences in beliefs that help make Mexico such an interesting place. Remember, though, that these small and apparently insignificant differences in everyday life are only the tip of the iceberg. Many other aspects of Mexican culture and life are also very different to Canada and the U.S.—not better, not worse, just different!

Sources / further reading

Chapter 1 The Three Sisters and early kitchens

Barba, Luis A. 1986. "La química en el estudio de áreas de actividad", in *Análisis de Unidades habitacionales mesoamericanas y sus áreas de actividad*, edited by Linda Manzanilla, 21-39. IIA, UNAM, Mexico.

Bushnell, G.H.S. 1976. "The Beginning and Growth of Agriculture in Mexico". *Philosophical Transactions of the Royal Society of London*, 275 (936): 117–120. London: Royal Society of London.

Landon, Amanda J. 2008. "The 'How' of the Three Sisters: The Origins of Agriculture in Mesoamerica and the Human Niche". *Nebraska Anthropologist*, 110-124. University of Nebraska-Lincoln.

Manzanilla, Linda. (ed.). 1993. *Anatomía de un conjunto residencial teotihuacano en Oztoyahualco*. 2 vols. IIA, UNAM, Mexico.

_____ 1996. "Soil analyses to identify ancient human activities". *Canadian Journal of Soil Science*.

_____ and L. Barba. 1990. "The study of activities in classic households. Two case studies from Coba and Teotihuacan." *Ancient Mesoamerica* 1: 41–49.

Millon, Rene 1973. *Urbanization at Teotihuacan, Mexico. Volume 1. The Teotihuacan Map: Text, Part 2. Maps*, University of Texas Press.

Somerville, A.D., N. Sugiyama, L.R. Manzanillo & M.J. Schoeninger. 2016. Animal Management at the Ancient Metropolis of Teotihuacan, Mexico: Stable Isotope Analysis of Leporid (Cottontail and Jackrabbit) Bone Mineral. PLoS ONE 11(8). http://journals.plos.org/plosone/article?id=10.1371/journal.pone.0159982 [16 August 2016]

Chapter 2 Ancient astronomers rebooted the calendar

Aveni, Anthony F. 1980. *Skywatchers of Ancient Mexico*. University of Texas Press.

Beltrán, Roberto S. 1975. *El Regreso de Quetzalcóatl*. Self-published. Mexico.

Garces C., Guillermo. 1990. *Pensamiento matemático y astronómico en el México precolumbino*. 2nd edition. Mexico: Instituto Politécnico Nacional, Mexico.

Morante, Rúben B. 1989. "La Gruta del Sol". *México Desconocido*, No. 147 (May), 17-20.

Chapter 3 Sustainable farming in Aztec times

Burton, Tony. 2013. *Western Mexico: A Traveler's Treasury*. Canada: Sombrero Books.

Rojas R., Teresa(coord) 1995. *Presente, pasado y futuro de las chinampas.* Mexico DF: Ciesas/Patronato del Parque Ecológico de Xochimilco A.C.

Sluyter, Andrew. 2002. *Colonialism and Landscape, Postcolonial theory and applications.* Rowman and Littlefield.

Chapter 4 Pyramid sounds and Maya blues

Arnold, D. E., J.R. Branden, P.R. Williams, G.M. Feinman & J.P. Brown. 2008. 'The First Direct Evidence for the Production of Maya Blue: Rediscovery of a Technology.' *Antiquity.* 82 (2008): 151–164. https://www.academia.edu/3518683/ [30 May 2016]

Lubman, David. 1998. "Archaeological acoustic study of chirped echo from the Mayan pyramid at Chichen Itza, in the Yucatan Region of Mexico... Is this the world's oldest known sound recording?" *Lay Language Paper,* 136th Meeting of the Acoustical Society of America. http://acoustics.org/pressroom/httpdocs/136th/lubman.htm [30 May 2016]

Martin, Simon, K. Berrin and M. Miller. 2004. *Courtly Art of the Ancient Maya.* London: Thames & Hudson.

Wikipedia entry. New7Wonders of the World - https://en.wikipedia.org/wiki/New-7Wonders_of_the_World [30 May 2016]

Chapter 5 Rubber balls and Americas' oldest ballgame

Hosler, Dorothy, S. Burkett and M. Tarkanian. 1999. "Prehistoric Polymers: Rubber Processing in Ancient Mesoamerica", *Science,* 18 June 1999.

Rochin, Robert, F. Solis and R. Velasco. 2010. *Ulama: El Juego de la Vida y la Muerte. Ulama, the game of life and death.* Estado de Sinaloa/Universidad Autónoma de Sinaloa http://www.ulamagames.com/book.html [11 March 2016]

Chapter 6 Roman symbols on a Maya pyramid?

Corliss, William R. 1995. "The inscribed bricks of Comalcalco". *Science Frontiers* #99 (May-June 1995). http://www.science-frontiers.com/sf099/sf099a01.htm [30 May 2016]

Fell, Barry. 1990. "The Comalcalco Bricks: Part 1, the Roman Phase," Epigraphic Society Occasional Papers, 19:299-336.

Steede, Neil. 1994. "The Bricks of Comalcalco," *Ancient American,* 1:8, Sept/Oct.

_____ 2012. *A Partial Translation of the "2012" Comalcalco Brick.* http://www.earlysitesresearchsociety.org/2012-comalcalco-brick.html [30 May 2016]

_____ and D.J. Eccott. 2001. "Comalcalco: A Case for Precolumbian Transoceanic Contact." *Migration and Diffusion,* Vol 1, #5.

Winters, Clyde. Undated. *Bilingual Mayan-Olmec Text.* http://www.geocities.ws/Athens/Academy/8919/biling.htm [30 May 2016]

Chapter 7 Post-conquest inventory

Acuña, Rene. (ed) 1987. *Relaciones geográficas del siglo XVI: Michoacán.* Volume 9 of *Relaciones geográficas del siglo XVI.* Mexico City: Universidad Nacional Autónoma de México. [translation by the author]

_____. (ed) 1988. *Relaciones geográficas del siglo XVI: Nuevo Galicia*. Volume 10 of *Relaciones geográficas del siglo XVI*. Mexico City: Universidad Nacional Autónoma de México.

Franco, Pedro. 1996. Introduction to "Breve relación del Nuevo Reino de Galicia y provincia de la Nueva Vizcaya de don Alonso de la Mota y Escobar" in *Descripciones* #15. Guadalajara: El Colegio de Jalisco.

Chapter 8 Oldest winery in the Americas

Casa Madero website. Undated. *Historia*. http://www.madero.com.mx/historia/#

Chapter 9 Baaad sheep depleted environment

Chevalier, F. 1987. *Land and Society in Colonial Mexico*. University of California Press.

Ciudad Real, Antonio de. 1993. *Tratado curioso y docto de las grandezas de la Nueva Espana: Relacion breve y verdadera de algunas cosas ...* 3rd edition. Mexico: UNAM Instituto de Investigaciones Historicas. Vol I, 28-29, 34; Vol II, 85, 86-90.

Diamond, J. 1998. *Guns, Germs and Steel*. New York: W.W. Norton & Company.

Hunter, R.W. 2009 "People, Sheep, and Landscape Change in Colonial Mexico: the Sixteenth Century Transformation of the Valle del Mezquital", *PhD dissertation*, LSU Dept. of Geography and Anthropology, May 2009. http://etd.lsu.edu/docs/available/etd-04022009-230601/unrestricted/Hunterdiss.pdf [10 October 2009]

Lázaro de Arregui, Domingo. 1621. *Descripción de la Nueva Galicia*. Edited by François Chevalier. Sevilla, 1946.

MacLachan, C.M. and J.E. Rodriquez O. 1980. *The Forging of the Cosmic Race: A Re-interpretation of Colonial Mexico*. University of California Press.

Melville, Elinor G. K. 1994. *A plague of Sheep. Environmental consequences of the conquest of Mexico*. Cambridge University Press.

Simon, Joel. 1997. *Endangered Mexico: An Environment on the Edge*. San Francisco: Sierra Club Books.

Chapter 10 Afro-Mexicans outnumbered Spaniards

Bakewell, Peter J. 1971. *Silver Mining and Society in Colonial Mexico: Zacatecas, 1546-1700*. Cambridge University Press.

Callaloo. 2006. *Callaloo (A Journal of African Diaspora Arts and Letters)*. The Spring 2006 issue, vol 29, #2, pp 397-543, has a series of articles under the general heading of "Africa in Mexico".

Green, Lance D., J.N. Derr, and A. Knight. 2000. "mtDNA Affinities of the Peoples of North-Central Mexico". *American Journal Human Genetics*. March, 2000. Vol 66(3): 989–998.

Restall, Matthew. 2003. *Seven Myths of the Spanish Conquest*. Oxford University Press.

Vaughn, Bobby. 2006. "Black Mexico Home Page, Afro Mexicans of the Costa Chica." *Mexconnect*. http://www.mexconnect.com/articles/1936 [30 May 2016]

Vinson, Ben, & B. Vaughn. 2004. *Afroméxico*. (translation by Clara García Ayluardo) Mexico: CIDE/CFE.

Chapter 11 Epic journeys and mythical cities

Balderrama Gómez, Roberto. Undated. *El Fuerte en la Historia*. Privately published.

Chapter 12 The Manila Connection: cultural exchange

Guevarra, Rudy P. 2011. "Filipinos in Nueva España: Filipino-Mexican Relations, Mestizaje, and Identity in Colonial and Contemporary Mexico" in *Journal of Asian American Studies*, 14:3, October 2011, 389-416

Mercene, Floro L. 2007. *Manila Men in the New World: Filipino Migration to Mexico and the Americas from the Sixteenth Century*. UP Press.

Chapter 13 Birth of the Mexican Navy

Verne, Jules. 1964. (Edited by I.O. Evans) *Dr. Ox and Other Stories*. (Includes "A Drama in Mexico"). Arco.

_____. 1876. "Un Drame Au Mexique. Les premiers navires de la marine Mexicaine". (E-text prepared by Christian Sánchez). http://jv.gilead.org.il/sanchez/mexique.html [30 May 2016]

_____. 1999. (Edited by Peter Costello) *Jules Verne: The Eternal Adam, and other Stories*. (Includes "The First Ships of the Mexican Navy"). Phoenix.

Chapter 14 U.S. appropriates Cinco de Mayo

Anon. Date unknown. "Cinco de Mayo – The Battle of Puebla, 1862". Republished online at http://geo-mexico.com/?p=10741 [30 May 2016]

Barker, Nancy N. 1979. *The French Experience in Mexico, 1821-1861. A History of Constant Misunderstanding*. University of North Carolina Press.

Vanderwood, Paul. 2000. "Betterment for Whom? The Reform Period: 1855-1875", in *The Oxford History of Mexico* (edited by Michael C. Meyer and W.H. Beezley). Oxford University Press.

Chapter 15 Railroads helped forge the nation

Campbell, Reau. 1899. *Campbell's New Revised Complete Guide and Descriptive Book of Mexico*. Chicago.

Carson, William E. 1909. *Mexico: the wonderland of the south*. New York: Macmillan.

Márquez Martínez, Teresa and Lucina Rangel Vargas (coordinators). 2010. "Estaciones Ferroviarias De México. Patrimonio Histórico, Cultural Y Artístico". Conaculta.

Chapter 16 Utopian experiment in Sinaloa

Anon. *Topolobampo Collection*. Fresno State University. http://www.fresnostate.edu/library/subjectresources/specialcollections/topolobampo.pdf [30 May 2016]

Moreno Rivas, Manuel. 1992. *Socialismo en Topolobampo, apuntes para la historia*. Editorial Agata, Guadalajara, Mexico.

Reynolds, Ray. 1996. *Cat'spaw Utopia, Albert K. Owen, the Adventurer of Topolobampo Bay and the Last Great Utopian Scheme*. Borgo Press, San Bernardino, California.

Robertson, T.A. 1964. *A Southwestern Utopia. An American Colony in Mexico*. Ward Ritchie, Los Angeles.

Chapter 17 Historic aerial bombing of warship

Cooper, Ralph. Undated. "Gustavo Adolfo Salinas Camiña, aka Gustavo Salinas Camiña, 1893-1964." http://www.earlyaviators.com/esaligus.htm [9 March 2016]

Freudenthal, Elsbeth E. 1947. "How Aviation "Firsts" Took Place in Mexico." *The Americas*, Vol. 4, No. 1 (Jul., 1947), 100-107

Villard, Henry Serrano. 1968. *Contact! The Story of the Early Birds*. New York: Thomas y Crowell Company, as quoted at "Moisant's Cross-channel Flight, 1910" http://www.earlyaviators.com/emoisjo1.htm [9 March 2016]

Chapter 18 Deceptive national symbols

Anon. 1996. "El Grito: Mexico's Cry for Independence". *Gaceta Consular*, Year IV, Number 25, September 1996. Mexico's Consul General in Austin Texas. Republished at http://www.mexconnect.com/articles/2825 [30 May 2016]

Duverger, Christian. 1987. *El origen de los aztecas*. Editorial Grijalbo.

González Block, Miguel A. 2004. "El Iztaccuahtli y el Águila Mexicana: ¿Cuauhtli o Águila Real?", *Arqueología Mexicana*, XII, 70: 60–65.

Krauze, Enrique. 1997. *Mexico: Biography of Power*. Harper Collins.

Chapter 19 Huichol Indians preserve traditions

Barrin, Kathleen (ed). 1978. *Art of the Huichol Indians*. The Fine Arts Museums of San Francisco.

Mata Torres, Ramón. 1980. *La Vida de los Huicholes. Tomo I*. Guadalajara, Jalisco.

_____1980. *El Arte de los Huicholes. Tomo II*. Guadalajara, Jalisco.

Neurath, Johannes. 2003. *Pueblos Indígenas del México Contemporáneo: Huicholes*. Comisión Nacional para el Desarrollo de los Pueblos Indígenas / UN Development Program. 2003.

Chapter 20 The Tarahumara of the Copper Canyon

Bennett, W. and Zingg, R. 1935. *The Tarahumara. Univ. of Chicago Press*. Reprinted by Rio Grande Press, 1976.

Kennedy, J.G. 1978. *Tarahumara of the Sierra Madre; Beer, Ecology and Social Organization*. AHM Publishing Corp, Arlington Heights, Illinois. Republished, as *The Tarahumara of the Sierra Madre: Survivors on the Canyon's Edge* in 1996.

Lartigue, F. 1970. *Indios y bosques. Políticas forestales y comunales en la Sierra Tarahumara*. Ediciones de la Casa Chata # 19, Mexico.

Merrill, W.L. 1988. *Raramuri Souls – Knowledge and Social Progress in North Mexico*. Smithsonian Institution, Washington D.C.

Nauman, T. 1997. "Tala ilegal para la siembra de mariguana y opio en Chihuahua" p. 50 in *El Financiero*, May 12, 1997.

Pennington, C. 1963. *The Tarahumar of Mexico, their environment and material culture*. University of Utah Press. Reprinted by Editorial Agata, Guadalajara, 1996.

Shoumatoff, A. 1995. "The Hero of the Sierra Madre", in *Utne Reader* (July-August 1995, 90-99, reprinted from *Outside*, March 1995.

Chapter 21 Train drive sacrificed life for town

Cross, Carolyn. 1912. "The American Cross of Honor", in *San Francisco Call*, 112: 114, 22 September 1912.

Dedora, Don and B. Robles. 1976. *Goodbye García Adiós: the true and powerful story of one of Mexico's authentic heroes*. Northland Press.

Laux, Peter. 2007. "Famous Mexicans on their Stamps: Jesús García, The Hero of Nacozari" http://www.mexconnect.com/articles/699 [30 May 2016]

Chapter 22 Archbishop who had miraculous birth

Anon. 1895. "Professor Frederick Starr", *The Salt Lake Herald*, 16 Nov 1895

Ellis, David. 1997. *D. H. Lawrence: Dying Game 1922-1930: The Cambridge Biography of D. H. Lawrence*. Cambridge University Press.

García Villa, Juan Antonio. 2004. "Dos anécdotas", *El Financiero*, 8 October 2004.

Parmenter, Ross. 1984. *Lawrence in Oaxaca: a Quest for the Novelist in Mexico*. Salt Lake City: G.M. Smith.

Serafín Sodi, José Antonio. 1978. Untitled biography of Thomas Gillow and Eulogio Gillow: http://botnav.webcindario.com/Biografia/ChautlaEx.htm [12 Feb 2016]]

Schlarman, Joseph. 1951. Mexico: A land of Volcanoes. Bruce Publishing Company.

Chapter 23 Cross-dressing maid conned high society

Anon. 1945. "Society of Dupes", in *Time Magazine*, 10 December 1945.

Cervantes Morales, Luis. 1969. *Memorias de Don Carlos Balmori escritas por su secretario particular: 23 de junio de 1926-27 de noviembre de 1931*. Costa-Amic.

Cottrell, John. 1979. *The Great Cities: Mexico City*. Time Life International.

García Bergua, Ana. 2005. "Y Ahora Paso a Retirarme: Balmoreados", in *La Jornada Semanal*, 560, 27 November 2005. http://www.jornada.unam.mx/2005/11/27/sem-ana.html [30 May 2016]

Hilton, Bernard. 1950. "The Deceptive Millionaire", in *True*, June, 1950; 27:157; reprinted in 1955 in *Grand Deception: A selection from the World's Most Spectacular and Ingenious Swindles, Hoaxes & Frauds*, edited by Alexander Klein. Ballantine Books.

Ortega Morán, Arturo. 2005. "Balmoreada", http://cvc.cervantes.es/el_rinconete/anteriores/marzo_05/22032005_01.htm [12 Feb 2016]

Robleto Hernán. Undated play. *Los millones de don Carlos Balmori*.

Chapter 24 Eccentric painter led art revolution

Casado Navarro, Arturo. 1984. *Gerardo Murillo, el Dr. Atl*. UNAM.

Helm, MacKinley. 1941. *Modern Mexican Painters*. Harper & Brothers.

Luna Arroyo, Antonio. 1992. *Dr. Atl*. Salvat.

Zuno Hernández, José Guadalupe. 1976. *Atl: Pintor y poeta*. Universidad de Guadalajara.

Chapter 25 Violinist added notes to musical scale

Anon. 1963. "The Musical Revolution of Don Julián Carrillo", *The Times*, 26 March 1963, 15.

_____ 2016. "Julián Carrillo y el sonido 13" http://www.sonido13.com/contacto.
html [12 Feb 2016]

Martínez, J.R., and S. Palomares-Sánchez. 1996. "Sonido 13: un paso hacia el infinito
musical" http://www.smf.mx/boletin/Jul-96/articles/son13.html [30 May 2016]

Solís Winkler, Ernesto. Undated. *Julian Carrillo and the Thirteenth Sound, a microtonal
musical system*. http://paginas.tol.itesm.mx/campus/L00280370/julian.html

Chapter 26 January's weather fortells year ahead

Adame Martínez, Homero. 2002. "Las cabañuelas, conocimiento emprírico del clima".
México Desconocido No.299, pp. 26-34.

Aparicio de Andrés, Divina. 1978. *Las cabañuelas*. http://www.alcozar.net/etnografia/
cabanuelas.htm [30 May 2016]

Minaya, Graciela. 1945. "Las cabañuelas y su origen". Originally published in *La Nación*.
http://www.acqweather.com/cabanuelas.htm [30 May 2016]

Chapter 27 World's most popular romantic song?

Cruz Barcenas, Arturo. 2005. "Murió Consuelo Velázquez". *La Jornada*, 23 January 2005.

Foxjan, Margalit. 2005. "Consuelo Velázquez Dies; Wrote 'Bésame Mucho.'" *The New
York Times*, 30 January 2005.

Chapter 28 Mexico's soundscapes and traffic whistles

Foris, David and Wilfrido Flores. 2016. *Chinanteco de Sochiapam*. SIL International.
http://www.mexico.sil.org/es/lengua_cultura/chinanteca/sochiapam_chinantec
[6 June 2016]

Gaceta Oficial. 2015. "Reglamento de Tránsito del Distrito Federal". *Gaceta Oficial,
Distrito Federal*. 17 August 2015. http://www.consejeria.df.gob.mx/portal_old/
uploads/gacetas/0dfe0f2c2728da104e72f26974d2ad23.pdf [6 June 2016]

Chapter 29 Sports fans embrace Mexican wave

Anon. 2008. "Giant Honeybees Use Shimmering 'Mexican Waves' To Repel Predatory Wasps". *ScienceDaily*. https://www.sciencedaily.com/releas-
es/2008/09/080909204550.htm [14 February 2016]

Farkas, I., D. Helbing and T. Vicsek. 2002. "Mexican waves in an excitable medium",
Nature 419 (2002), pp. 131-2. Supporting website, "Mexican wave: Crowd behaves
as excitable medium" at http://angel.elte.hu/wave/ [14 February 2016]

Guinness. 2016 *Guinness World Records*. http://www.guinnessworldrecords.com/world-
records/longest-mexican-wave-%28timed%29 [14 February 2016]

Chapter 30 Mexican cats have only seven lives?

Sellers, Jeff M. 1994. *Folk Wisdom of Mexico*. San Francisco: Chronicle Books.

Toor, Frances. 1947. *A Treasury of Mexican Folkways*. Crown Publishers.

Winter, Evelyne. 1968. *Mexico's Ancient and Native Remedies: A Handbook of Testimoni-
als and Historic References for Modern Use*. Mexico City: Editorial Fournier.

Acknowledgments

Several of the chapters in this book are based on articles first published on http://mexconnect.com. I am very grateful to Carol Wheeler, formerly Mexconnect's Chief Editor, and to David McLaughlin, Mexconnect's publisher, for their long-standing support and encouragement.

The title is a nod to Norman Pelham Wright whose collection of essays entitled *Mexican Kaleidoscope*, published in 1948, was an eye-opener for me when I first began to get intimately acquainted with Mexico more than forty years ago.

Chapter 22 was significantly enhanced by family history material graciously shared by Archbishop Gillow's great granddaughter, Patricia Dormire. I am grateful to Thom Smith of Boca Raton, Florida, for alerting me to the likelihood that Estación Wadley was named for William Wadley, one of his ancestors.

My sincere thanks to Dr. Julian Fell and the Epigraphic Society for permission to reproduce the image used in chapter 6.

Among the many people who have helped shape this book, I owe a special debt of gratitude to my wife, Gwen, and to Jim Brown, Celia Burton, Marisa Burton, Trevor Burton, Michael Hogan, William Kaliher and Loy Strother.

Index

V

Vaca, Alvaro Nuñez Cabeza de, 56
Valens, Richie, 53
Valle de Mezquital, 46-48
vanilla, 2, 60
Vargas, Pedro, 145
Vaughn, Bobby, 52
Velasco, Luis de, 47
Velázquez, Consuelo, 145-149
Venezuela, 155
Veracruz, 3, 24, 26, 27, 49, 51, 52, 53, 63, 65, 70, 74, 75, 82, 85, 92, 116
Verne, Jules, 67-71
Villa, Pancho, 60
Villahermosa, 33
Villard, Henry, 92
vineyards, 39, 41, 42
Vinson, III Ben, 52
violence, 109
violinists, 135
Virginia, 88
Virgin of Wine, 43
Voisin biplane, 92
volcano, 42
volleyball, 25
vulcanization, 27

W

W (the letter), 80
Wadley, 80
warning shouts, 164
War of Independence, 95, 119
warship, 91
water rights, pollution, 14, 87
weather, 141
weeds, 46
Weller, Rob, 157
Welles, Orson, 148

Western Sierra Madre, 85, 86, 101, 113
Western State, 55, 58, 59
wheat, 38, 46
whistles, 152, 154
wine, winery, 39-43
Winters, Clyde, 31, 32
wolves, 38
World Bank, 110
World Cup (soccer), 157, 159
World Fair, St. Louis, 114
World Fair, London., 120
World Heritage, 11, 15, 25
Wright brothers, 91

X

Xalapa, 82
XEQ, radio station, 147
Xochicalco, 7, 8, 9, 10, 11, 70
Xochimilco, 15
xylophones, 53

Y

Yaqui Indians, 57
yarn artwork, 102, 104
Yecapiztla, 82
Yucatán (state and peninsula), 17, 20, 30, 52, 80, 82
Yucatán Peninsula, 17, 20, 30, 80

Z

Zacatecas, 39, 51, 101, 104, 116
Zacatula, 70
Zamora, 37
Zapotec, 8
Zaraga, 132
Zaragoza, Ignacio, 75, 76
zeppelins, 91

Illustrations

With the exception of the image of masons' marks in chapter 6, all illustrations are the original work of Mexican artist Enrique Velazquez.

The drawing for Chapter 13 is based on a 1896 painting of the *Asia* by Angel Cortellini Sánchez.

The depiction of the biplane in chapter 17 is based on the photograph of Captain Gustavo Camiña and his biplane *Sonora* reproduced on Ralph Cooper's website, as referenced in the chapter notes.

The remaining illustrations are based on photographs taken by the author, images believed to be in the public domain, or derive from the artist's imagination.

The illustrator

Born in Guadalajara in 1947, illustrator and watercolorist Enrique Velázquez studied drawing and painting at the Escuela de Artes Plásticas of the University of Guadalajara. His watercolor work shows the influence of renowned Jalisco watercolorist Alfonso de Lara Gallardo and of American painters Bruce McGrew and Larry Watson.

Enrique and his wife, Belva, also an artist, have had a joint studio on Calle 16 de Septiembre in Ajijic, Jalisco, since 1990. Enrique's watercolors are in private collections throughout North America. He has also painted numerous murals, including those decorating La Nueva Posada hotel in Ajijic, and designed several book covers.

For more information about the art of Enrique and Belva Velázquez, and their annual art calendars, please visit their website at mymexicoart.com

The author

Tony Burton, born in the U.K. in 1953, is a geographer who taught, lectured and guided specialist cultural and ecological trips in Mexico for 18 years.

He has written extensively on Mexico's history, economics, tourism and geography, and won ARETUR's annual international travel-writing competition for articles about Mexico on three occasions. His work has been published in numerous magazines and journals in Mexico, Canada, the U.S., Ireland and elsewhere.

His previous books include *Western Mexico: A Traveler's Treasury* (2014), now in its fourth edition, and *Lake Chapala Through the Ages, an Anthology of Travelers' Tales* (2008). His cartography includes the best-selling *Lake Chapala Maps*, first published in 1996. Tony is the co-author, with Dr. Richard Rhoda, of the landmark volume *Geo-Mexico, the Geography and Dynamics of Modern Mexico* (2010).

Tony and his wife, Gwen, live on Vancouver Island in Canada and frequently travel back to Mexico.

The author can be contacted via geo-mexico.com.

Other books by this author

Western Mexico: A Traveler's Treasury (4th edition, 2014)

"One factor that lends special appeal to this singular travel book is Burton's departure from the stock formula found in conventional guides. He adheres to a more organic approach, drawing on personal experience and meticulous research to divulge the virtues and peculiarities of every destination."

- Dale Palfrey for the *Guadalajara Reporter*, 2014

Lake Chapala Through the Ages, an Anthology of Travelers' Tales (2008)

"Intermingled with the first-hand accounts of the area in different eras, Burton provides snippets of background history to give some larger context and enhance the reader's overall understanding of this particular region and Mexico in general... Burton is a consummate scholar whose writing is also enjoyable to read."

- novelist Robert Richter on Amazon

Geo-Mexico, the Geography and Dynamics of Modern Mexico (2010) (co-authored with Richard Rhoda, PhD)

"Geo-Mexico illustrates both the richness of geography as a field of study and the spectrum of cultural, economic, and environmental anomalies that make Mexico so eternally fascinating . . . I highly recommend this volume to educators, students, and anyone with more than a passing interest in the culture, history, terrain, economy, politics, or development of the country."

- Felisa Rogers for *The People's Guide to Mexico*